For Carl, Anna and Mark

Front Cover illustration: (outer) the runic neck-ring from Pietroassa, Rumania, bearing the text **gutaniō wi(h) heilag** *"hereditary possession of the Goths, sacred, holy"; (inner)* the Leeds runic fragment.

RUDIMENTS OF RUNELORE

Stephen Pollington

Anglo-Saxon Books

BY THE SAME AUTHOR

Wordcraft
An Introduction to the Old English Language & its Literature
The Warrior's Way

Published 1995

Published by
Anglo-Saxon Books
Frithgarth
Thetford Forest Park
Hockwold cum Wilton
Norfolk England

Printed by
Antony Rowe Ltd.
Chippenham
Wiltshire
England

A Catologuing-in-Publication record for this book
is available from the British Library.

ISBN 1–898281–16–5

CONTENTS

ILLUSTRATIONS

PREFACE

My purpose in writing this book is to provide the person coming fresh to the subject of runes with a handy and inexpensive reference work such as I would have wished to have when I began studying the ancient languages of the north, some twenty years ago.

The situation today is very different from then, however: I had to comb the second-hand bookshops of London to find a couple of not very reliable treatments of the subject, whereas today there are large numbers of books about runes and more appearing every year. The usefulness of any book is not always apparent since the subject has strayed into the hands of occultists and professional scholars, and the interested, non-specialist layman is likely to feel reviled by both parties! I hope to have gone some way to redressing that situation, and to have provided "the man on the Clapham omnibus" with as much sound and unbiased information as he can be expected to want to make use of. A short bibliography gives my main sources for this present work, although my other actual sources are the many works on more or less closely related topics I have consulted over the years and the not inconsiderable time I have spent trying to work out the details of the inscriptions, either at first hand or from photographs.

The bulk of the present book comprises the text "Rudiments of Runelore" a much expanded version of a talk given in the winter of 1994 to a London meeting of The English Companions. The further sections entitled "The Norfolk TIW Runes" and "The Brandon Runes" were prepared for publication in another format until the opportunity presented itself, at the suggestion of Tony Linsell of *Anglo-Saxon Books*, to include them with other relevant material to produce a comprehensive but manageable book devoted to the subject. I also include the texts of the more commonly referred to *Rune Poems*, with my own translations, for ease of reference.

It is to be hoped that this book will prove useful and informative to those with an interest in the old northern traditions of the English and their former neighbours. To that end, I have avoided detailed argument based on scholarly works of philology or archaeology as the size and scope of this book do not warrant such treatment (the few less 'accessible' aspects can safely be ignored at the first reading); I have nonetheless made use of some technical literature, and tried to present the findings of others in an intelligible way – whether successfully or not you must judge for yourself.

My thanks are due to Alan Haymes for drawing my attention to many of the less accessible articles consulted in preparing this work, to Janice Baker for her help and support, and to Tony and Pearl Linsell for their patience in tackling the production of this book.

Steve Pollington
Essex, January 1995

8

ONE

ChE RUOIMENCS OF RUNELORE

RUNES The word conjures up all sorts of pictures and can be used in a number of different ways. To some people it recalls the dread practices of the bloody Teutons, scoring their mystic sigils on stock and stone to summon or to ward off the hags and hedgeriders, witches and valkyries, wild huntsmen and warlocks of the northern night. To others it represents the arcane manuscript traditions of mediaeval Europe, the cryptographic markings of secret science and lore, hidden from the intellects of the uninitiated and made the more mystical for having been set into otherwise comprehensible texts, so tantalizing in their not-quite-accessibility. Perhaps far more people today may know of the runes through the mock-mediaeval world of Professor Tolkien, whose imagination was fired by tales of great deeds in times past, and secrets of unguessed ages lying disregarded and mouldering in the imaginative sterility of librarianship. Again, some few may have heard and read of the current 'New Age' re-appraisal of northern European heritage, and have been privy to runic posturing and meditation or 'occult secrets of the Celtic runemasters'.

One thing is common to all these meanings of the word 'rune' – they all suggest antiquity and secret learning; those which are not 'magical' in the strict sense nevertheless retain a certain glamour of the ancient and the arcane. Runes are *old*, always belong to a past world, and they always evoke those secrets of initiation – sometimes sinister, sometimes merely obscure – which attend the mention of the word. In this book, I propose to look at the runes themselves, their origins, what they were used for and how they were used.

But before we look at runes and runelore in some detail, let's follow a common sense approach and try to find out what the truth is about the beginnings of the subject. What exactly are runes? I suppose a textbook answer to that question would have to say that they are 'a Northern European writing system developed primarily for carving on wood, horn or other organic material, and consisting of simple, straight lines in a limited set of formal combinations'. This gets us started, but doesn't really take us very far. For a start, runes are by definition associated with Germanic-speaking peoples like the English, Germans and Scandinavians; I shall be returning to 'Celtic runes' below, but for now it will suffice to limit our view to the mainstream of the subject. Secondly, runes are primarily a purely practical tool; they have the functions of both letters and signs – can be used to spell words or to stand for words – but at no time were they ever regarded as mere decoration or ornament. (Perhaps I should qualify that by saying 'at no time until the present century ...'). Thirdly, the runes as we can now perceive them are not the *rūna* of Old English manuscripts, or *rúnar* of the Norse; contemporary attitudes to the signs are unrecoverable, and we cannot know now what went through a Saxon's mind when he saw the characters or heard the word. (In fact, even the word 'rune' went out of use in this sense, and was re-introduced from mediaeval Latin; had the Old English word survived, it would have the form 'rown', just as the rhyme-word *tūn* is now spelt 'town'.) All we can do is interpret what we can discover in the light of what seems likely or reasonable to us today, without the possibility of certainty. Anyone who speaks dogmatically about runelore is on very thin ice.

Rūn is an Old English word, signifying 'mystery, secrecy, hidden knowledge' used of men sitting apart to mutter and whisper together as well as of messages passed between them by means of writing. There are cognate forms in some Celtic languages, e.g. Irish, although there the meaning of 'secret' was retained without the sense development to 'runic character used for writing'. When the Irish came to devise their own script, typically they came up with something more like a code than a set of letters, the Ogham. The idea of secrecy attached to writing is not new, of course: to those not in on the secret, all communication not open to public scrutiny appears at least slightly sinister.

The Origin of the Runes

The history of runes is not easy to trace and there are probably at least two paths to tread: one starts back in the Bronze Age in Northern Europe, perhaps in the second or third millennium BC in southern Scandinavia. Here there are a great many rock-carvings depicting scenes from contemporary life: the hunt, seafaring, various types of ritual (including what is almost certainly a form of ritual pairing or marriage), warfare and possibly some mythical events. Around and within the carvings are a variety of simple geometric signs, comprising circles, dots, crosses, hooks and zigzags; combinations of various elements produce symbols such as spear shapes, ladders, swastikas, trees and spirals.

The second path begins in the southern Alps, where an existing alphabetic script, based on Etruscan writing and used to record one or more North Italic dialect, was adapted to the sound system of Germanic by a person or persons unknown. This was presumably in the second century BC, since the classical Latin script was adopted in this region not long after that. The composite system which was developed from the combination of Scandinavian symbols and North Italic alphabetic characters is known as the *Common Germanic Fuþark* or rune-row and comprises twenty-four distinct characters:

Ϝ	⋒	▶	Ϝ	ᚱ	ᚲ	ᚷ	ᚱ
f	u	th	a	r	k	g	w
ᚺ	ᚤ	I	ᚦ	ᛃ	Ψ	ᛈ	ϟ
h	n	i	y	ǣ	z	p	s
↑	ᛒ	ᛗ	ᛘ	ᛚ	◇	ᛝ	ᚷ
t	b	e	m	l	ng	d	o

Figure 1
Common Germanic Runes
with their approximate English sound values
– see below for more details.

The Greek-based system of writing is called an *alphabet* after the first two letters of the series, *alpha* and *beta*; similarly, as you can see, the Germanic rune-row is called a **fuþark** after the first six of its characters. So far, no-one has found a satisfactory explanation for the order of the runes in their sequence, although it does seem to have been fixed from earliest times since it varies little during the entire period of the script's use. The suggestion has been made that the first five runes of the English variant (f.u.þ.o.r.) represented an acronym of *fæder ūre þū on rōdre* which is an approximate rendering into Old English of "Our father which art in heaven", though few would accept such a proposal today!

The runes' angular appearance is due to the materials on which they were intended for carving: wood, bone and horn. It is possible to analyse these rune-shapes in terms of distinctive features, but unfortunately no underlying principles of sound representation appear (e.g. all the vowels or dental consonants having a common feature), although their construction is evidently based on a system of variable oppositions: most runes consist of an upright, called a 'stave', and at least one crosspiece. They can be summarized as in Appendix 1.

Each character has a sound value and, if later evidence is to be trusted, a name beginning with that sound (insofar as the language allowed). All the names were nouns and many were culturally significant or emotionally charged words which would certainly assist in making the script memorable in purely mnemonic terms and also meaningful in symbolic terms. The names of these Common Germanic runes were nowhere recorded, but later versions from England, Scandinavia and Iceland assist us in making deductions about the originals. Nevertheless, it has to be remembered that some of the names, and to a greater extent the 'meanings' or 'interpretations' of the names, are based on scholars' best guesses and are not entirely dependable.

Runes among the Germans

Before we look at the characters themselves, there is one aspect of runic origins which has been little commented on but deserves mention. The runes are a Germanic script, and indeed the earliest known records of any

Germanic language are the runic amulets and so forth of the Jutland peninsula and the surrounding Scandinavian areas. The language so recorded is a very early form of North West Germanic, perhaps a literary dialect in which specific local features had been suppressed (just as we today don't record our actual speech in the fixed and formal spellings of our written language). Now the earliest Germanic prose texts of any length are the biblical translations of Bishop Wulfilas into his native Gothic in the fifth century AD, in a Greek-based script of his own devising; why did he not simply use runes for his writings? The answer may be that he, and the rest of his folk, did not use them. The Goths are believed to have begun their migration out of Scandinavia in the second century AD, and to date there is only one piece of evidence which can be said to link them with the use of runes, namely the Rumanian neckring from Pietroassa which bore a runic text, one interpretation of which is 'Hereditary Possession of the Goths, holy, sacred'. Without this single item, or rather this interpretation of it, the earliest runic texts all seem to be from Jutland and thereabouts, and in the language we associate with that region, namely the ancestor of the North Sea Germanic languages (one of which is English) and of Norse. The probability seems to be that runes were developed in that area and that the Gothic neckring (if such it be) represents a cultural export to the east.

It could be argued that the Goths' own runic traditions had died out under the influence of Greek culture – and this remains a possibility, supported by the fact that the names of some of the Gothic characters are reminiscent of rune names, e.g. the 'f' character is called '*fe*' and the 'h' '*haal*'. But if certain rune-shapes and their corresponding names were taken over from designs used in the Bronze Age rock-carvings, the Goths may actually have recorded an older layer of nomenclature than the runic tradition. The problem in deciding lies in the dating of the earliest runic pieces, which are conventionally ascribed to the period AD 250-400 by art historians; the dates given are said to be supported by linguistic evidence, though in fact it seems that the linguists have decided on dates in the first few centuries AD on the basis of art-historical writings. In other words this is a circular argument – historians deriving dates from linguists whose dates are derived in turn from historians. All that can safely be said is that the runes were already in wide use in the early centuries AD, and their use apparently began in the Jutland peninsula. This may be significant, since it was from just this region that the Roman legions drew many of their Germanic mercenaries, and the early Germanic rune-bearing amulets (called *bracteates*) are evidently copies of Roman coins and medallions. As this area is known to have been under strong Roman influence in the Early Roman Iron Age, there is every likelihood that the use of runes on Germanic jewellery represents a native reaction against Roman script which was (and is) ill-suited to the writing of the Germanic dialects. The weak link in using this argument to account for the origins of the script is that the runes themselves are not drawn straight from Roman capitals or any known form of cursive script, but seemingly from the North Italic script in use in the Alps; looking a little further back in history, though, we have the great northern Germanic triumphs over Rome of the *Cimbri* and *Teutones* in the last centuries BC, whose passage included Alpine areas where the Italic script flourished. The *Cimbri* have left their name in the island of *Himmerland*, off the Jutland coast. The angular i.e. 'runic' form of writing may thus have been in use there since those times, though being scratched into perishable materials it has not survived archaeologically, and only the Roman impetus on the Germans towards increased use of more permanent materials, and greater use of writing generally, has preserved this evidence for us.

Perhaps even more interesting (for us) is the fact that the peoples of the Jutland peninsula were dominated by a group of seven tribes whose main distinguishing feature was (according to informed contemporary Roman opinion) the worship of a mother goddess called *Nerthus* – among whom, one group, the *Anglii,* were later to emigrate westwards to the ex-Roman province of Britannia and establish a powerbase there.

The Germanic Rune Row
and the Common Germanic Language

The provisional or reconstructed Germanic rune names are set out below with their Old English and Old Norse counterparts. The English and Scandinavian names are recorded in manuscripts of the Christian period, in the form of 'Rune Poems' in which each character is the subject of a verse; the poems agree fairly well with each other as to the names and meanings, and in some cases even contain similar phrases or ideas which may mean that they have come down from an ancient original – though it could also be that the Norse material was imported at the time of the Danish invasions. There are omissions from the Scandinavian sources due to simplification, reducing the number of characters from 24 to 16 – obviously some names were discarded with their referents. I shall point out important differences in the meanings in these separate traditions when relevant. The division into groups of eight (Icelandic *ættir*) is traditional and plays a part in runic cryptographic systems, as we shall see.

Runic spelling is not entirely regular, lacking the discipline which printing, word-processing and mass literacy demand. The runes were conventionally written from left to right, but the earliest inscriptions are commonly written from right to left as well. In fact, it is not at all unusual for longer runic texts to be written *boustrophedon*, which is to say alternately left-to-right and right-to-left. Some runemasters reversed their letter-shapes when writing right-to-left, for example the word '(he) swam' which would have the form XI4rFᛗM in left-to-right format appears thus:

Figure 2
Detail from the Franks Casket front panel
the word 'giswom' with retrograde characters.

while others inverted them alternately, e.g. the word 'brother' (ᛒᚱᚢᚦᚢᚱ) in a Danish inscription:

Figure 3
Detail from stone inscription at Helnæs, Fyn, Denmark
the word 'bruþur' in inverted characters.

In the following section, there are certain special characters used to show sounds for which modern English spelling has no separate letters. These are as follows:

j   in Germanic texts has the sound value we attribute to 'y' as in 'year'

ŋ   this sound would be spelt -ng- in modern English, as it is the nasal consonant after the vowel in words like *song, fang, thing, lung*; it normally occurs when 'n' precedes 'k' or 'g' e.g. 'thinker', 'finger'.

þ   we now spell this sound 'th' in words like 'thigh', 'thin'

ð   this sound is also spelt 'th' as in 'thy', 'thine'

ƀ   a sound no longer in use in English, something like a 'v' but pronounced with the lips only (not the teeth and lips)

χ   this sound occurs in some dialects of English, for example in Scots words such as 'loch'; it is pronounced like a 'k' but instead of ending in a sharp release of air, the sound vibrates in the throat and is released slowly

ǣ   a long vowel pronounced in the front of the mouth, similar to that in English 'had', 'rag', etc.

γ   another sound no longer used in English, it is the equivalent of χ pronounced with the voice, so that its starting point is a 'g' sound

ā etc.   a line above a vowel indicates that it is pronounced 'long'

It should also be noted that the asterisk (*) before the words given below means that they are 'reconstructed', which is to say that they represent forms so ancient that they are not recorded anywhere but have been deduced from words found in the later, recorded languages. OE means Old English, OIc means Old Icelandic, ON means Old Norse, West Saxon is a dialect of OE, as is Anglian.

(Refer to the relevant Rune Poems on pp. 46–67.)

FIRST GROUP

ᚠ

*fehu
(sound value 'f')

the reconstructed Proto-Germanic word for 'cattle, moveable wealth', (one of our words for money, 'fee') here perhaps representing the bovine with its horns protruding, although the influence of the Latin capital F is also evident in the shape of the character. The bovine is known to have been a cult animal among the early English, of whom Tacitus says that they worshipped Mother Earth under the name *Nerthus*, whose processional waggon was drawn by cows. The English and Norse use of the rune restricts the meaning to 'wealth', the notion of 'livestock' having been lost from the later languages; in some passages, OE *feoh* has overtones of 'princely treasure' with all the associations of ancient glory and personal honour the Germanic peoples valued so highly.(OE *feoh*, ON *fé*)

ᚢ

*ūruz
(sound value 'u')

probably the word for the *aurochs*, a large species of primitive cattle against which Germanic youths used to test their courage and skill at arms; it may have a transferred meaning 'manhood, vigour' on this account. The horns of the beast were much-prized, and from them drinking vessels were made by the addition of elaborate metal fittings. Fine examples were unearthed from mounds at Sutton Hoo (only the fittings survived) and the Taplow barrow. The aurochs was not found in England in Anglo-Saxon times, so the retention of the word with this sense underlines the Anglo-Saxon regard for ancient traditional lore. The Norsemen substituted a homonym meaning 'drizzle'. (OE *ūr*, ON *úr* 'drizzle', OIc *úr* 'slag') þ

*þurisaz

(sound value 'þ')

is a kind of large, malevolent being often translated as 'giant' although perhaps 'demon' or 'wizard' are closer to the original idea; this rune-name was altered in Anglo-Saxon England to *þorn* 'thorn' on account of its shape, and taken over into the bookhand to represent the sound 'th' (Þ, þ). The OE verse is skilfully worded and may still have echoes of the original meaning, since it is possible to detect indirect references to a kind of maleficent creature who prays on human frailties. (ON *þurs*)

F

*ansuz

(sound value 'a')

is the word for a member of the family of the gods, whom the Norse call the *Æsir*; it may refer here especially to *Wōden*, the god with special runic links. The OE poem has replaced this with the homonym '*ōs*' (mouth) though there is a strong possibility that there is a punning reference to Wōden, the god most closely associated with eloquence and prophecy, in the cleverly worded verse. The English rune F continued in fourth place even though a character with the same shape (F) remained in use with a different sound value. This suggests that the runes were remembered mainly by their names, and that *ōs* continued to occupy the position of its ancestor ***ansuz**. (OE *ōs*, ON *óss*)

R

*raiðō

(sound value 'r')

is the act of 'riding' or where this takes place, the 'road'; the two modern senses have split from the original single idea of 'road' as wherever one chooses to ride. This rune may have been used as a journey charm, like a modern 'St. Christopher' medallion, or to speed the dead on the road to Hel. Many Anglo-Saxon funerary urns feature heavy 'chevron' decoration which may reflect a group of r-runes in series. (OE *rād*, ON *reið*)

‹
*kaunaz/*kēnaz
(sound value 'k')

meaning uncertain, either 'ulcer' or 'torch'; most modern rune books favour the latter since the element of fire is otherwise lacking from the rune-row, but linguistically there is a good case for either form – it is to some extent the modern passion for order and notion of four elements which militates for 'torch'. Yet the OE name *cēn* has the meaning 'firebrand', although this does not seem to have been a common word in the language. (OE *cēn* 'torch, firebrand', ON *kaun* 'ulcer')

X
*gebō
(sound value 'ɣ' or 'g')

is the 'act of giving' as well as the thing given, whether a bestowal on a fellow or a sacrifice to the gods. Gift-giving was a central theme in Germanic culture, creating bonds of mutual loyalty and obligation throughout society which helped to hold communities together and to make links between distant parts of Germanic Europe. Warriors were publicly honoured at feasts where they were presented with gifts of land, treasure, wargear and items of personal equipment as a mark of their success, loyalty and worth; the giver, by inference, also increased his prestige by proving himself willing and able to bestow magnificent gifts. (OE *gyfu*)

ᚹ
*wunjō
(sound value 'w')

can be rendered 'joy' or 'pleasure' although it also has connotations of affectionate relationships (OE *wine* 'friend') and mutual support (OE *winnan* 'fight'). With ***gebō** it encompasses all manner of bounty and freedom from want, the protection of one's kindred and the pleasure of human contact. The rune was adopted into the bookhand as p, Þ where it served to represent the sound we spell with 'w'. The OE poem gives the name as *wen* which is a word for 'hope' or 'expectation', but the following verse and other evidence suggest that ***wunjō** is the true original. (*Wen* could also conceivably represent the English form of the name of the deities whom the Norsemen worshipped under the name *Vanir*, but there is no known evidence for their worship under that name among the English.) (OE *wen*)

SECOND GROUP

ᚺ   ***hagalaz**

(sound value 'χ' or 'h')

is 'hail', which the English, Icelandic and Norse Rune Poems all refer to as a kind of 'grain'; it is the first of the so-called winter-runes. In the English tradition, this verse opens the second octet of runes and is longer than the standard three-line set, perhaps to mark this transition. (OE *hægl*, ON *hagal*)

ᚾ   ***nauðiz**

(sound value 'n')

means 'need, distress' (and may be a euphemism for 'death'); it is the antithesis of the rune ***wunjō**. OE verse describes *nȳd* as *wyrda heardost* 'the hardest of events' and its range of meanings seems to cover all kinds of physical privation and negative emotion. The OE poem presents it as a kind of adversity which may act as a test of moral fortitude. (OE *nȳd*, ON *nauðr*)

ᛁ   ***īsaz**

(sound value 'i')

is 'ice', a fitting partner for ***hagalaz** and the last winter-rune before ***jēra** 'spring'. In Germanic tradition, ice was the primeval solid matter from which everything else was created or released through the action of its opponent, fire. Here we may see a link with the power of runes to bind or freeze, just as ice freezes and locks creation in its grasp. The OE poem stresses the beauty and marvellous quality of ice, rather than its harmful aspects. (OE *īs*, ON *ís*)

ᛃ   ***jēra**

(sound value 'j')

is the 'year' both as the measure of time and also as the passing round of seasons from springtime to harvest, but excluding the winter months. It has strong associations with the land's fertility and with fruitful harvests. (OE *gēr*, ON *ár*)

ᛇ   ***eihwaz**

is a puzzling rune about which there is still no agreement as to the meaning or the sound value; the English evidence suggests a sound 'ih' or 'iχ' and meaning 'yew tree'. The most plausible original sound value is *ǣ*, since this sound occurs in Germanic and no other rune has that value, but the confusing nature of the few occurrences of this character make it very difficult to decide whether this is tenable or not. The yew, which was more usually called *īw* or *ēow* in OE, was especially connected with protection and rune-magic, however. The reference to the tree as *hyrde fȳres* 'fire's keeper' is cryptic and may reflect the use of the tree as firewood, as the Norwegian *Rune Poem* suggests, or perhaps the use of containers of yew wood for transporting smouldering embers (a birch bark pannier was used for this purpose in the early Bronze Age). (OE *ēoh*)

ᛈ   ***perþ-**
                                   (sound value 'p')

is far and away the most enigmatic rune, partly because its sound value was a rarity in Germanic. The OE *Rune Poem* mentions something which is a pleasure to men in the hall and various suggestions from 'dice box' or 'chessman' to 'sexual relations' have been put forward but none has been generally accepted. An interesting speculation is that the shape represents the primeval well of past time which periodically overflows when an age of the world passes, at which time the world-tree shakes and cataclysmic events take place on earth – the *ragnarokr* or passing of the mighty ones – as movingly described in the Icelandic poem *Voluspá*. However, there is also the possibility that *peorþ* is merely a rhyming doublet of *cweorþ*, the name of the later, English 'q'-rune, and that both are taken over from some Celtic original, perhaps connected with *ceirt*, the ogham name for the apple tree. (OE *peorþ*)

*algiz
(sound value 'z')

is the presumed form for this rune which occurs in the Old English *Rune Poem* in a confusing verse about a kind of sedge and in the Norse with the meaning 'bow'. However, the sound 'z' which the original represents was dropped in early Old English and changed to a variant of 'r' (written 'R') in Norse, so both languages can be assumed to have remodelled their runic traditions accordingly. The Norse name *ýr* (bow made of yew) is based on *eihwaz (see above) while the Anglo-Saxons had no need of a special 'z'-rune since the early English language only used the sound as a pronunciation variant (allophone) of 's'; the value 'x' was transferred to the character in Christian times. The original meaning is presumed to have been 'protection, guard', a word which gave rise to OE *ealgian* 'to protect' and the word *ealh* 'temple, sacred place' (see p.75f. below). That there may also have been a connection with the name *Alcis,* cited by Tacitus as applied by the Germanic folk to a pair of divine twins, cannot be excluded either, given that their worshippers regarded them as especially concerned with saving those in danger, much like the Greek *Dioskouroi.* (OE *eolhsecg,* ON *ýr*)

*sōwulō
(sound value 's')

means 'sun' which both English and Norse traditions reflect. It has been proposed that OE *sigel* 'sun / 's'-rune' (and also *swegel* 'sky') refer to a sun cult represented by the sun symbol ⚡; there can be no doubt that the sun played a central role in most early European religion. It was sometimes conceived of as a huge radiant disk borne on a waggon or ship across the vault of heaven – hence the seafaring imagery of the OE poem.(OE *sigel,* ON *sól*)

22

THIRD GROUP

*teiwaz

(sound value 't')

is the name of the principal Germanic god of the early heathen period, before *Wōðenaz* usurped his position (his name is equivalent to Roman Jupiter and Greek Zeus). While not simply a war-god, the spear-symbol which stands for his name suggests masculine associations – arms were the mark of the freeman in early Germanic society, allowing full participation in legal and social matters; this symbol is taken over directly from the Bronze Age rock carvings. The English verse refers not directly to a heathen god but to a constellation, though native Germanic religion had an astrological dimension just like the Roman and Greek. The rune may well have been used as a victory charm, and it is found on various weapons, funerary urns and amulets with obvious apotropaic intent. (OE *tīr*, ON *Týr*)

*berkana

(sound value 'ƀ' or 'b')

has the literal meaning 'birch-tree' although its associations are rather with fertility and spring rites (the birch is often the first to sprout leaves and catkins in the northern forests). The OE poem describes a tree more like an aspen than what we call a birch. (OE *beorc*, ON *bjarkan*)

*ehwaz

(sound value 'e')

is the horse and the rune's shape may represent the legs and bent back of the creature. The horse was a sacred animal among the German tribes, and was used for divination and sacrifice, though the OE poem refers rather to the human joy in horses and their usefulness to man. Norse has lost this rune. (OE *eoh*)

ᛗ

*mannaz
(sound value 'm')

means 'man' or 'mankind' and may be linked to the divine ancestor *Mannus* (***Mannuz**) mentioned by the Roman writer, Tacitus. The OE verse stanza tells of man's social role and his fallibility and mortality, which is a long way from any notion of divinity. (OE *mann*, ON *maðr*)

*laguz
(sound value 'l')

is 'water': either the substance or with the more specific meaning 'body of water, lake', possibly connected with the ritual waterscapes of Jutland where sacrifices were made to the gods. The passage of time among the early Germanic peoples was conceived of as a stream which would periodically overflow – see ***peorþ** above -and there is certainly an ambivalent attitude to the sea and seafaring in most early Germanic literature, commanding both affection and respect. (OE *lagu*, ON *logr*)

◇

*inguz
(sound value 'ŋ')

represents the divine hero, consort of the mother goddess and himself probably a vegetation spirit; this figure seems to have been the particular favourite of the Angles who may be the original 'friends of Ing (*Ingwine*)' though this name was retained by the later inhabitants of southern Jutland and may be recorded first by Tacitus in the form *Ingaevones*. The later Swedish kings called themselves *Ynglingar* which may mean 'scions of Ing'. The reference to the waggon in the OE verse may recall the cult processions of *Nerthus* where she represents Earth Mother who is wooed by the Green Man (*Inguz*) and who spends time visiting men's homes in a ritual waggon accompanied by a priest. (OE *Ing*)

*ðagaz
(sound value 'ð' or 'd')
means 'day' or 'daylight', although it has been dropped from the Norse rune-row. With ***sōwulō** and ***jēra** it may refer to symbols of a sun-cult, which the OE verse supports with its reference to every man's enjoyment of the sun's radiance. (OE *dæg)*

*ōþila
(sound value 'ō')
is often the last of the Common Germanic runes (although sometimes the last pair ᛗ and ᚧ are reversed), with the meaning 'inherited wealth, homeland, farm, family estate', which apparently complements and contrasts with the 'movable wealth' of the first rune. In OE, under certain conditions, *ō* was pronounced further forward in the mouth (and spelt *œ*) and ultimately became identical with *ē*, though the rune continued to be used as an ideogram for the word *ēþel* 'homeland'. (OE *ēþel)*

The Germanic runes set out above are adequate for the representation of the Proto-Germanic language, which has been carefully reconstructed by scholars working backwards from known languages such as English, Dutch, Danish, German and so on. The system of contrasting sounds (phonemes) worked out for the original language comprises sets of related values as follows:

Nasals:	m, n, ŋ
Liquids:	l, r, s, z
Semi-vowels:	y, w
Vowels:	short a, e, i, u
	long ē, ī, ō, ū, ǣ

In addition, Germanic had three sets of consonants which could be pronounced with or without the voice, as stops or as continuants (e.g. 'p' is voiceless, and 'b' is its voiced equivalent; if the 'p' sound is not pronounced with the lips fully closed, but with an escape of air, a sound closer to 'f' is produced – a so-called 'continuant'). In contrast to most modern Germanic languages, though, the reconstructed language had voiceless stops, voiceless continuants and voiced continuants:

Voiceless Stops	p	t	k
Voiceless Continuants	f	þ	χ
Voiced Continuants	ƀ	ð	γ

The voiced continuants seem to have had pronunciation variants (called *allophones*) from the earliest times, which are the sounds we would recognize as 'b', 'd', 'g'. These were not separate sounds in the original language, however. Similarly, χ became 'h' through the development (or retention) of this sound as an allophone.

If we now compare the above system with the runic evidence, we find that the twenty four sounds coincide remarkably well with the *fuþark*:

m, n, ŋ	ᛗ ᛏ ᛜ
l, r, s, z	ᚱ ᚱ ᛋ ᛦ
y, w	ᛃ ᚱ
a, e, i, ō̄, u, ǣ	ᚠ ᛘ ᛁ ᛉ ᚢ ᛄ
p, t, k	ᚲ ᛏ ᚲ
f, þ, χ	ᚠ ᚦ ᚺ
ƀ, ð, γ	ᛒ ᛗ ᚷ

One point of divergence does exist, however: conventionally, 'ŋ' is not considered a separate sound but merely the allophone of 'n' occurring before 'k', 'g'. Nevertheless, the development of a separate rune for this sound does suggest that the native users of the language regarded it as a discrete phoneme which warranted a character of its own.

Incidentally, Germanic is believed to have had an additional set of consonants pronounced with rounded lips (like 'q' in 'queen' versus 'k' in 'keen', where the principal difference is the rounded lips needed to form the 'q' sound). However, there is no evidence for any special runes set aside for Germanic '*χw*', '*kw*' or '*γw*' which rather suggests that to native speakers at least the spellings ᚺᚱ ᚲᚱ ᚷᚱ were an adequate representation of these sounds.

As an example of the Common Germanic *fuþark* in use, we may take the text from one of the Illerup shield mounts:

Figure 4
Inscription from silver shield mount
Illerup, Jutland, Denmark.

This inscription is interesting for two reasons: firstly, the text is retrograde and the runes are reversed accordingly; secondly, some of the runes have been deliberately cut to be read both ways, e.g. ⋫ for the more usual ▶ 'th'. The text reads **ediwat ojiþin** which reverses to form **niþijo tawide** "Nithijo made (this)" (Nithijo is a woman's name).

The English Runic Tradition (see also the OE Rune Poem pp.51–5)

The specifically English innovations to this system are of two types: the 'common' adaptations which took place during the English settlement (5th and 6th centuries AD) and the more restricted 'northern' additions from Northumbria in the 8th century.

The commonest form of the English rune-row, called a *fuþorc* to distinguish it from the Germanic and Norse traditions, can be set out thus:

Anglo-Saxon Futhorc

ᚠ	ᚢ	ᚦ	ᚩ	ᚱ	ᚳ	ᚷ	ᚹ
f	u	þ	o	r	c	g	w

ᚻ	ᚾ	ᛁ	ᛄ	ᛡ	ᛇ	ᛈ	ᛋ
h	n	i	(j)	(ih)	(x)	p	s

ᛏ	ᛒ	ᛖ	ᛗ	ᛚ	ᛝ	ᛞ	ᛟ
t	b	e	m	l	ŋ	d	œ

ᚫ	ᚪ	ᛠ	ᚣ	ᛥ	ᛢ
æ	a	ea	y	st	q

27

Obviously many of the English forms are direct developments from the Germanic originals, which themselves varied in shape over the period of their use. The common English innovations are:

the use of the Germanic a-rune ᚠ for the sound spelt in Old English *æ* (the vowel in 'cat');

the use of the Germanic ō-rune ᚪ for the sound spelt *oe* in Old English; this sound later became *e* in standard West Saxon, and the rune fell into disuse as there was already a rune for the sound (ᛗ);

the use of the Germanic z-rune ᛏ with the value 'x' (mainly a later development under the influence of the manuscript tradition)

certain characteristic English rune shapes, mostly extending the more irregular characters to full height:

ᚻ is reshaped with staves extended ᚺ

◊ is reshaped with extensions ᚼ

ᛇ is remodelled round a single stave ᛝ

ᛉ has the forms ᚢᚱ

and new runic forms such as:

ᛠ is named *ēar* and has the sound in Old English of the diphthong 'ēa'; the word *ēar* has at least three meanings in OE. The first, 'sea', is related to the Old Icelandic word *aurr* 'water' and the second, 'earth', to the Old Icelandic *eyrr* 'sandbank'; the third, 'ear of corn', is connected with Old High German *ahar* 'spike'. Discounting this latter meaning, the OE rune could refer either to the grave, or to a watery death at sea. In either case, the finality of the verse rounds off the OE Rune Poem satisfactorily.

ᚣ is *ȳr*, the 'yew bow'; it has the sound value 'y' ('i' pronounced through rounded lips) and is transparently a combination of ᚻ and ᛁ. There is a Norse rune of the same name, based on the *algiz original.

ᚩ   is the new 'o'-rune **ōs**, (the direct descendant of *ansuz) as the old 'o'-rune ᚫ changed its sound to 'œ'.

ᚠ   **āc** 'oak (tree)' has the value 'a' in English as the old 'a'-rune ᚠ took on the sound 'æ' due to changes in the language; the verse stanza shows different aspects of the tree in man's service as provider of acorns and, once built, as a ship.

ᛥ   occurs in both English and Frisian texts with the value 'st' and is called **stān** (stone).

ᛢ   is found as a runic 'q' although Old English had no particular need for such a character, hence this may be another development from manuscript practice.

The later (mainly Northumbrian) forms are:

ᛇ   is called **ior** or **iar** but its exact meaning is unknown – it may be a development of the Nordic 'j'-rune **jár** before it became **ár** in recorded Norse texts. The OE verse refers to some sort of amphibious creature, possibly an otter.

ᚻ   **calc** is a special modification of ᚲ the English 'c'-rune, itself modified from ᚲ and standing for a variant of 'c' before a front vowel.

ᚸ   **gār** denotes the variant of 'g' between back vowels.

ᛣ   denotes a variant of 'k' (name unknown)

We can compare the OE rune row with the sounds actually used in the language (standard West Saxon variety), as we did for Germanic above.

Continuants:	f þ ð χ h
Stops:	p t c ċ
	b d g ġ
Liquids:	s ſ z r l
Nasals:	m n ŋ
Semivowels:	j, w

Vowels: short   a æ e i o u y œ

             long   ā ǣ ē ī ō ū ȳ œ̄

(Diphthongs in Old English are very complex and not easily treated in a summary such as this.)

The sound represented by 'ċ' is a palatal variant of 'c' similar to the sound we spell 'ch' (e.g. 'church'); 'ġ' represents a palatal 'g' similar to the sound we spell 'j' or 'dg' (e.g. 'judge'); ſ is the sound spelt 'sc' in Old English and 'sh' in modern English (e.g. 'ship').

As can be seen, the English runes fit this system quite well although the redundant rune ᛉ was not entirely abandoned; it still occurs in manuscript sources at least as an ideogram for *ēþel* 'homeland'. It is obvious, however, that 'x' and 'q' were not needed as the sounds could be represented by 'cs' and 'cw' respectively, as they usually were in manuscript orthography (*æcs* 'an axe', *cwic* 'quick, alive').

As an example of English runes in use, we may take part of one panel from the front of the Franks casket, which bears the following text:

Figure 5
Detail of the front panel of the Franks Casket.

The runes read **hronæsban** which can be split into two OE words having the standard West Saxon spelling *hrones bān* 'whale's bone' which is the material from which the casket is made.

The Scandinavian Runic Tradition (see also the Norwegian and Icelandic Rune Poems pp. 58–62)

The Norse runic tradition diverged from that of western Europe in that, instead of creating new runes to reflect new sounds, the Scandinavians actually reduced the number of signs to sixteen. There are two slightly different versions of the Scandinavian rune row (*fuþǫrk*), one in use in Denmark and the other in Norway and Sweden.

It is a curious fact that Iceland, which did more than any other nation to preserve the indigenous traditions of the north, including knowledge of runic practice, has hardly a runic inscription to its name, save the very late material from the High Middle Ages.

The Danish rune row, divided in its three *ættir*, is set out below. It should be noted that, although the number of separate runes decreased, the sound system of the Norse languages went through a process of development so that an increased range of sounds had to be represented by a smaller character set. This strange contradiction makes the reading of northern inscriptions unnecessarily difficult and problematical: many runes have to represent several sounds each, so that interpreting a Norse text is a matter of fitting the possible sounds to the runes and seeing if a word emerges! Briefly, the vowels are represented only by 'u', 'i', 'ǫ' (an 'a' pronounced nasally) and 'a'; runes for sounds which may be pronounced with or without the voice may represent either value (↑ may be 't' or 'd'). As an example take these names from Harald Bluetooth's runic monument at Jellinge (':' represents the double-dot word separator used in many runic texts):

transcription	'normalized' spelling	English
haraltr : kunukR	*Haraldr konungr*	Harold (the) king
kurmfaþur	*Gorm faþur*	Gorm (his) father
þaurui : muþur :	*Þorve moþur*	Thyra (his) mother
nuruiak	*Norveg*	Norway
tanmaurk	*Danmark*	Denmark

A representative Danish *fuþǫrk* is as follows:

ᚠ	ᚢ	ᚦ	ᚬ	ᚱ	ᚴ
f	u	þ	ǫ	r	k

ᚼ	ᚾ	ᛁ	ᛅ	ᛋ
h	n	i	a	s

↑	ᛒ	ᛘ	ᛚ	ᛦ
t	b	m	l	R

31

The Swedish/Norwegian rune row is broadly similar, although the runes for 'h' and 'm' have been merged, as well as 'b' and 'f', while 's' and 'R' are reduced to a half-height stroke:

ᚠ	ᚢ	ᚦ	ᚨ	ᚱ	ᚴ
f	u	þ	ǫ	r	k

ᚼ	ᚾ	ᛁ	ᛅ	ᛌ
h	n	i	a	s

ᛏ	ᛒ	ᛘ	ᛚ	ᛦ
t	b	m	l	R

In the light of the multiple readings possible with the reduced system, the inadequacy of the sixteen rune sequence for normal communication purposes was soon evident, and the Norsemen consequently introduced the addition of a dot to the stem of the more ambiguous characters:

ᚴ	k	ᚵ	g, ŋ
ᛁ	i	ᛂ	e
ᛒ	b	ᛔ	p
ᛏ	t	ᛐ	d

Runes persisted longer in use among the Scandinavians than elsewhere, and were carried by Vikings to Iceland and Greenland (and according to some, to North America also, though that is at best doubtful). Here is part of the most northerly runic inscription found so far, that from Kingiktorsoak, Greenland, dating from the early 1300's:

Figure 6
First line of the inscription from Kingiktorsoak, Greenland.

Some idea of the difficulties faced by the runologist can be gained from an examination of this text, first as transliterated from the stone, then in expected Old Icelandic form:

[the meaning of the first sign is unknown]
el/likr.sikuaþs.so/n:r.ok.bian/ne:tort/arson:

(The notation 'x/y' means that both 'x' and 'y' appear on one stem as bind runes – see below.) This would appear in more normal Old Icelandic as "Erlingr Sighvatsson ok Bjarni Þorðarson" the names of two of the persons who set up the stone. At this stage in the language's development, the sound written 'R' (the Norse development of Germanic 'z' written ᛦ) has merged with the other 'r' sound (developed from Germanic 'r' ᚱ) since here ᚱ is used erroneously as a flexional ending.

There are far more texts in Scandinavian runes than in either the Common Germanic or English ones, which has made Scandinavia the centre of runology worldwide, and the student of the subject will sooner or later come up against the need to familiarize himself with the Nordic material. Fortunately, the far-ranging Vikings erected runestones all over their world, from Russia to Ireland and even scratched a short text on the shoulder of the lion statue which used to stand in Piraeus harbour (it is now in Venice), recording the deeds of a fallen comrade. Nevertheless, it is not necessary to go to Scandinavia for this as there are Norse runes scattered across Britain from London to Orkney.

Runes and Pseudo-runes

Due to their angular character and their very limited resources for variation, runic texts are sometimes indistinguishable from random scratches produced by wear and tear on the surface of an object. This is especially so with portable items such as funerary urns and belt fittings. Many inscriptions, particularly the earlier ones, are lightly incised into the surface of the object and it is really very difficult, even when we believe a text to be present, to determine which scratches are intended to form the runes and which are due to chance or mistakes in cutting. A case in point is the inscription from the Gilton sword pommel:

Figure 7
Runes from the Gilton, Kent sword pommel.

It is apparent that these marks are too numerous and deliberate to be mere wear and tear, but interpreting them is no easy task especially as the upper edge of the inscription has been worn away. It seems safe to say that the character resembling a '3' is a retrograde 's'-rune and that the marks after it are 'i', 'g', 'i' and 'm'; if the next can be read as a rune for 'æ', the next looks pretty much like an 'r' and the whole seven letters can be convincingly read as the personal name *Sigemǣr* (earlier **Sigimǣr*). The other runes are barely legible, however, and R. W. V. Elliott's reading **eicsigimernemde** "eic sigimer nemde" (Sigimer named (the) sword) is a brave (and optimistic) attempt to resolve the puzzle.

Equally, some angular decoration and symbols can be interpreted as runic even when there is no overriding reason to do so. It is therefore prudent to be cautious, and to consider all possibilities rather than seeing every lozenge-shaped motif as an invocation of the god Inguz!

It is perhaps worth stressing that runes are most definitely <u>not</u> associated with any Celtic-speaking folk of antiquity, despite the fanciful Victorian invention of so-called 'Celtic' alphabets with more than a passing resemblance to the *fuþark*, for example the *Coelbren Y Beirdd*. The inspiration for this fabrication was a kind of misplaced nationalist zeal which insisted that 'anything the Sasnaig did must have been copied from the British, who had done it earlier and better'. In fact, the Celtic languages were first recorded in a variety of Mediterranean scripts and the first home-grown writing system seems to have been the Ogham of Ireland.

Rune-like characters were used by a people of the Asian steppe of Turkic affinity, and by the speakers of early Hungarian, but no direct connection with the Germanic letters is to be sought. The fact that the systems were used for similar purposes on similar materials accounts for the angular character of both sets of signs.

The Uses of Runes

What were runes used for? There are two answers to this question: namely (1) writing and (2) magic. Neither is wrong but nor is either the whole truth. The uses of runes from the earliest inscriptions suggest that their purpose was for writing short formulae of very specific types. As an example we could cite the very early text 'makija mariða ala' from the sword-chape found in the bog at Vimose, Fyn, Denmark; it means 'Alla decorated (the) sword' and is reasonably interpreted as a maker's mark of a type which occurs regularly wherever runes are used. Or we might look at the roughly contemporary clasp from Gardlosa, Skane, bearing the text 'ekunwoðz' which seems to be 'I (am) Unwōðz'. These short texts appear to be merely prosaic records for identification purposes. However, it is possible to look at the wording in a different light and read into it something a little more significant. In the first example, the verb 'mariða' can mean both 'decorated' and 'made famous or prestigious', which could conceivably be a sort of written formula recording the charming of the sword in order that it serve its user well. In the second example, the word 'unwōðz' could be a personal name (or nickname) meaning 'the peaceful' but this is not a plausible name for a cloak-fastener. More likely is the use of this runic text to protect the wearer against mental anxiety or divine possession – 'wōðz' is the battle-madness which affects berserks and also the 'altered perceptual state' experienced by the diviner, the seer and the poet. This quality was ascribed to a particular god whose name (Wō ðenaz, Wōden or Óðinn) is derived from it. The brooch thus acts as an amulet for the wearer against the spirits of possession. It is not difficult to see why runes are intertwined with magic and the control of supernatural forces when apparently innocuous inscriptions can be interpreted in such widely different ways.

Wōðenaz was the single god most closely connected with runes and their uses, and the Norse sources credit him not with their discovery or invention, but rather with having been ritually sacrificed rather like a shaman and while in the trance-like state, of having taken the runes from the branches of the world tree *Yggdrasill*. Interestingly, almost the only reference to Wōden in Old English literature (the *Nine Herbs Charm*) has the god using 'twigs of glory' (*wuldortānas*) to slay the serpent which has caused distress to the patient – a practice very reminiscent of the shamanic healer. Quite what this tradition should tell us about the origin of the script is hard to tell: that it is a gift to man from the gods? or that it is essentially part of the 'otherworld' entered by shamanic practices and should only be used by those initiated into those rites? Many of the early runic inscriptions are variants on the theme '*ek erilaz*' which means 'I (am) Erilaz' and one may legitimately ask: what does this mean? what was an 'Erilaz' and why was the fact of being one worth recording? The name is conventionally associated with the tribe known to the Romans as the *Heruli* and to the *Bēowulf* poet as the *Eorlas*; this derivation is not without its linguistic problems, and doesn't advance the argument a great deal since the Heruli (properly *Eruli*) were a people on the fringe of Germanic history, principally remembered for having remedied the miseries of senility and sickness by murdering the old and infirm. Their name has been taken as equivalent to the OE *eorl* 'hero' and ON *jarl* 'leader, earl' and more broadly as connected with words meaning 'vigorous, great' also found in the Germanic divine names *ermanaz* (applied to the sky-god *Tiwaz*) and *Erce* found in an OE charm for restoring health to the land (*Æcerbōt*). There is at least some *prima faciae* evidence to connect the assertion '*ek erilaz*' with membership of a rune-using society or brotherhood of the kind suggested by the ritual aspects of the early inscriptions.

Beyond this 'interpretational' reading of runic texts, there are an embarrassingly large number of inscriptions which consist of impossible verbal forms, such as the one on the Lindholm amulet from Skane:

'aaaaaaaazzznnn bmuttt: alu:'

which clearly isn't meant to be read as an alphabetic transcription of anything spoken. In such cases, we have to shrug and say that we don't actually know what this is supposed to mean. This doesn't mean that 'magic' is the only possible solution – and some people have been eager to find magic in runes wherever possible – but in the absence of a better working hypothesis it certainly seems to be the favourite. Like the archaeologists who cover their embarrassment at not being able to tell what an artefact is by giving it the blanket name 'ritual object', runologists have often been baffled by a text and declared it to be magical gibberish. There is, I think, a difference between 'supernatural' or 'magic' belief and the ritual or cult words and signs we find recorded in runes at all periods. Viewed in this light, the eightfold repetition of 'a' becomes comprehensible – all runic practice seems to favour the numbers three and eight (there are 3 x 8 = 24 runes, for a start) and the 'a' rune ᚠ stands for the word '*ansuz*', the generic name for any of the gods of the north. An eightfold invocation of the Germanic gods could be a powerful ritual tool. The thrice repeated 'z' rune ᛉ stands for '*algiz*' meaning 'defence, protection', another word with obvious apotropaic qualities, while the triple 'n' ᚾ stands for '*nauðiz*' or 'need'; overall the intention seems to be an invocation of the divine powers for protection against dire straits. The significance of '*bmu*' is unclear to me ('birch-tree' / 'human being' / 'aurochs') but the threefold 't' rune clearly marks an appeal to the god *Tīwaz* whose name is that of the rune. Finally, *alu* is a recognized protective formula of very frequent occurrence on runic objects.

Pausing here for a moment, it is worth noting that '*alu*' is an unusual and powerful word – I have suggested elsewhere (see below, pp.75f.) a link with the rune '*algiz*' meaning 'protection' and also, more distantly, with the word 'ale' (the drink) and ultimately with that 'otherness' experienced under the effect of ale, the 'hallucination', which is also related to the ancient root of these words. But '*alu*' was not an everyday word, as far as we can tell, and its use here may go back to very ancient and long-lived practice. I have detected it on an early cremation urn found here in England, and dating from the fifth century AD. A sceptic might argue that a Germanic formula like '*alu*' wouldn't mean anything to an Anglian settler in Britain because the Anglian (i.e. English) language had changed quite a lot between the time of these very early inscriptions and the Anglian migration. This is actually not a weakness but rather a strength of my argument, since amulets – if they are to inspire confidence – should be associated with things which are removed from the world of everyday experience. It makes them special, gives them religious or magical power, and sets them apart. Anyone who doubts this attraction of ritual, traditional and archaic language should look at current attitudes to sacred texts, whereby Roman Catholics retain their holy writings in Latin and Jews theirs in Hebrew; even many reformist Protestant sects prefer the King James Authorized Version of the Bible, which hardly reflects current linguistic usage. Furthermore, if an amulet is charged with the power of its runic inscription, then it becomes a tool for making things happen (if you want them to) or stopping them from happening (if you don't) – both ideas associated with Wōðenaz in his role as a personification of 'wish', later called by the Norsemen *Vili* or 'Will' and considered to be a brother (or hypostasis) of *Óðinn*.

How did the ancients use the script, then? This is a difficult question to answer, partly because we have no reliable outside eye-witness accounts of Germanic runemasters in action, and partly because what we deduce from the existing texts and descriptions is very much coloured by what we want to find there – the example of *'ekunwoðz'* above is a case in point. Tacitus, the Roman writer of the 1st century AD, describes the Germanic practice of consulting the omens, by scratching signs on twigs cut from a fruit-bearing tree and throwing them onto a white cloth, whence the officiant took three at random and drew his conclusions from the signs chosen. Now the text does not say that the signs used were runes, but it doesn't say they weren't either; therefore, those who wish to see runic sortilege in this passage are free to do so, citing as supporting evidence the previously mentioned *wuldortānas* 'glory-twigs' with which Wōden the rune-wielding god strikes in the *Nine Herbs Charm*.

To get a glimpse of runes in their natural habitat we have to wait a few centuries and move west a few hundred miles, to Britain in the time of Bede (i.e. the late 600s and early 700s). Bede tells the story of an Anglian nobleman called Imma who rode to war and had the misfortune to be captured by the enemy, who decided to sell him as a slave. Meanwhile, Imma's kinsman, a clergyman, believed him dead and began praying for his soul. Held bound awaiting transport to the slave-markets of London, Imma amazed his captors when his bonds fell from him – which Bede the devout Christian ascribed to the power of the prayers being said in his name. His captors, ignorant heathens that they were (implies Bede), wondered greatly at this and asked him if he knew loosening spells and had the runes written down about him. This episode is interesting in two ways: (1) because it shows that belief in the power of runes was credible behaviour, at least for heathens; and (2) because it links runes with the power to unbind. One of the more frightening aspects of the god Wōden/Óðinn was his power to 'bind' his foes with what the Norse called the *herfjottur* or 'army-fetter', a kind of desperate mental paralysis which could overcome even the mightiest in the thick of battle and render them unable either to defend themselves or even run away. (The prime meaning of the word *ansuz 'Germanic god' is possibly 'binder', according to some experts.) If this binding power could be harnessed by mortal magicians, then the prudent warrior would have amulets to protect himself from it, the "loosening runes" which Imma's captors believed him to have concealed about him.

Old English literature has more to say about runes, though sometimes the most revealing aspects are the most casual. Vocabulary is one area where the language occasionally drops its guard and shows runes in their natural state. Consider the following:

	literal translation	normal translation
gerūna	with – rune-r	counsellor, confidant
rūncofa	rune-chest	chamber of secrets, innermost thoughts
rūncræftig	rune-skilled	skilled in mysteries, the occult
rūnere	rune-r	whisperer, tale-bearer
rūnian	to rune	to whisper, murmur, tell secrets
rūnlic	rune-like	mystical, occult
rūnstæf	rune-staff	runic character
rūnwita	rune-knower	counsellor, adviser

This last seems to me to be one of the most telling items – a 'rune-knower' is a counsellor or adviser, suggesting that possibly every chieftain had amongst his ministers an appointed official whose business it was to 'know runes', to be able to use and interpret them. Similarly, the first word, 'one who exchanges runes' suggests either a sinister co-conspirator in some secret or, perhaps more optimistically, a kind of secretary sending state-secret messages, although whether by runic characters or by whispered instruction to the messenger is unclear. The poem *Bēowulf* shows us the Danish champion Unferþ, the king's favourite who has been overshadowed by Bēowulf and wants to cut him down to size with hostile speech; the poet says that he *beadurūn onband* 'unbound a battle-rune' i.e. began to act in a hostile manner, which suggests that declarations of hostilities were formally conveyed by a runic text, the uncovering of which signalled that peaceful relations should henceforth cease. Another text mentions *sittan sundor æt rūne* 'to sit apart at runes' which could either be writing a runic message or huddling together, whispering. One possibility is that wooden batons were carved with texts and used to send messages like modern letters, since certain riddles and at least one longer Old English poem depend on the literary device of the runic messages passed on in this way (*The Husband's Message*). Old Norse literature also mentions these artefacts, and the excavations under mediaeval Bergen in Norway actually brought a few to light; some were traders' tokens or ownership tags, though others bore simple messages. This prosaic, homely and unremarkable use of runes as a practical medium of communication argues for a widespread runic literacy in the north, as do some of the runic riddles in the Old English *Exeter Book*.

The Norsemen also knew various types of rune which could act as a charm and bring luck or ward off evil. In the *Hávamál* (Words of the High One) the god Óðinn, enumerating his many skills, says:

Þat kann ek it tólpta	A twelfth one (spell) I know
Ef ek sé á tré uppi	If I see upon a tree
váfa virgilná	a corpse dangling
svá ek ríst ok í rúnom fák	so I cut and colour in runes
at sá gengr gumi	so that that man walks
ok mælir við mik	and talks with me.

What kind of runes these were he doesn't say, but other texts refer to victory-runes, ale-runes, birth-runes, surf-runes, health-runes, speech-runes, thought-runes, fertility-runes, love-runes, battle-runes, and weather-runes. Truly, all human life is here, and there were seemingly runes for every occasion. The 'ale-runes' may actually be the inscription *'alu'* discussed earlier, while the 'victory-runes' could contain the rune *'tiw'* named for the god of warfare. The efficacy of the charm was increased (or the latent power unleashed?) by 'colouring' the runes with blood – the spell above says *i rúnom fák* 'I colour in runes' where 'colour' may refer to the god's blood or that of a sacrifice. Traces of bright pigment have been found on Scandinavian runestones, including the small memorial stone discovered in the churchyard of St. Paul's in London. Painting would have helped the text to stand out from its background as well as lending to the overall effect of the monument.

As a kind of postscript to the heathen Germanic runic lore, there are the manuscript runes of the later period, merging into the High Middle Ages. When the English came to record their own speech, they adapted the Latin alphabet to their needs but found it wanting in that there were sounds in English for which no Latin character was available. After experimenting with combinations of letters, someone somewhere had the idea of using the runic form corresponding to the sounds to be represented. The main problems were with the dental fricatives ('th' as in 'these' and 'thesis'), which were thus written with the thorn rune ᚦ modified for the bookhand as *þ*; similarly, the wen rune ᚹ was used for 'w'. (Incidentally, with the introduction of printing, the thorn character was remodelled as a 'y' so that the word 'the' (*þe*) appeared to be spelt 'ye' – hence such eccentricities as 'ye olde tea shoppe'.) Not content with this, Anglo-Saxon scribes occasionally used runes to stand for words, as in *Waldere* where *ealdne* ᛟ 'ancient homeland' is written with the *ēþel* rune acting as an ideogram.

In the Middle Ages, elaborate seriffed runes were used in manuscripts in England, Germany and Iceland with forms such as:

ᚠᚢᚦᚨᚱᚴᚷᚹ

Many of the riddles in the Exeter Book have runic clues embedded in their texts, e.g. number 19

ic on ſiþe ſeah ᛋᚱᚮᚻ *I saw on a journey SROH*

41

where the runes spell in reverse the word *hors* 'a horse'. Indeed, the English *Rune Poem* has a decidedly riddling quality in some verses, for example where *āc* is described as both the living tree and the ship made from the wood of that tree.

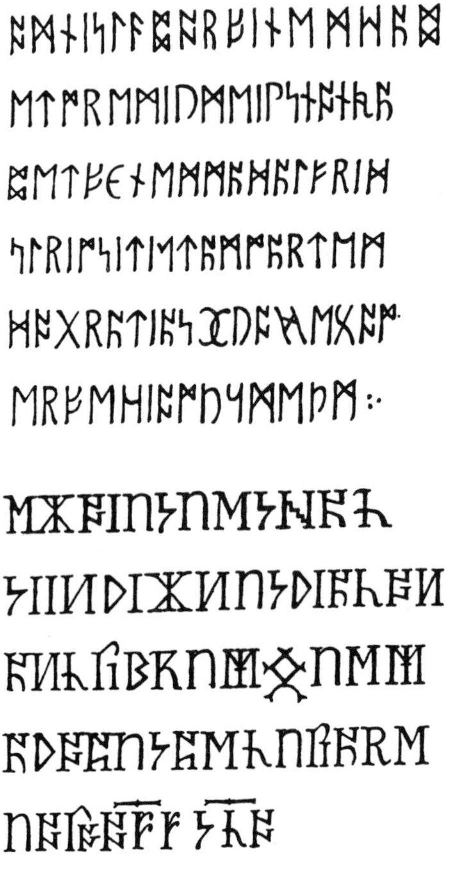

Figure 8
Runes from a MS. at Freisingen, No. iv 6
and the BL Harley MS. 1772 f.6v.

Bind Runes and Runic Cryptography

Two particular aspects of runic practice worth mentioning are *bind runes* and the various cryptographic systems used in both England and Scandinavia. Bind runes are groups of characters written in such a way that they form a single sign: examples of such would be the group 'dd' on an English grave stone, written as ⋈, the combination 'ga' ⋋ on some early Scandinavian finds and the character ⋢ 'on' from a Greenland Viking inscription. (see page 32, fig.6) One Frisian example is of a doubled 'st'-rune with the form ⬚. Some of the specifically English rune shapes are formed in this way: due to linguistic changes, many of the vowels of Old English were pronounced higher and further forward in the mouth due to the influence of the sound *i* and the runes themselves re-modelled as shown above.

The various systems in runic cryptography are based on the traditional division of the rune-row into three sets of eight runes each; using simple numerical indicators the writer can point to the set (called in Old Icelandic an *ætt*) and the position of the character within its set to identify it; for example the numbers 1:3 show the first *ætt*, third rune which is ᚦ(*þorn*). There are various ways of indicating the position, among the commonest are 'ice runes' e.g. ⊪⊪ (3:2 = ᛒ) 'twig runes' e.g. ↑ (1:1 = ᚠ) and *hahalrúnar* (pot-hook runes) e.g. ⅄ (2:1 = ᚺ). But with the introduction of these secret writing systems the vigour seems to have gone out of the script, which degenerated to an academic's plaything found mainly in manuscripts and monasteries. Quite complex systems were devised to disguise the crypto-runes, for example the number of spines on the back and belly of drawings of fish, or the whiskers in the beards of a series of stylized faces. The twig rune system was used to some extent in England, however, on monumental stonework, where the extended *fuþorc* meant that four *ættir* were needed. Even though the principle of the system is understood, there are still twig rune texts which have not so far been 'cracked' – partly due to the poor state of preservation, and partly to the way the encryption has been handled. Even on some fully legible texts the results of attempted decipherment are meaningless, which suggests that the community using these runes had developed a further secretive measure, perhaps counting from some point other than the left end of the row, or numbering the runes non-consecutively, or something equally devious.

two

FOUR RUNE POEMS

1. The Old English Rune Poem

The Old English *Rune Poem* is recorded in George Hickes's *Linguarum Veterum Septentrionalium Thesaurus*, (thesaurus of the languages of the old north), a printed book of 1705; whatever manuscript original Hickes was working from has not survived. The rune names appear to have been added later to an existing poem in which only the characters were given, and some at least are south-eastern dialect forms (e.g. *wen* for West Saxon *wynn*). Although it is difficult to make assumptions from a printed copy, the regularity of the verse suggests either an early date for the poem (e.g. ninth century) or a deliberately old-fashioned poem of somewhat later date.

 feoh byþ frōfur fira gehwylcum
sceal ðēah manna gehwylc miclun hyt dǣlan
gif hē wile for drihtne dōmes hlēotan

> *wealth is a comfort to any man / yet each person*
> *must share it out well / if he wants to win*
> *a good name before his lord*

 ūr byþ ānmōd and oferhyrned
felafrēcne dēor feohteþ mid hornum
mǣre mōrstapa þæt is mōdig wuht

> *aurochs is fierce and high-horned / the courageous*
> *beast fights with its horns / a well-known moor-treader,*
> *it is a brave creature*

45

ðorn byþ ðearle scearp ðegna gehwylcum
anfengys yfel ungemetum rēþe
mann gehwylcum ðe him mid resteð

> *thorn is painfully sharp to any warrior / seizing it*
> *is bad, excessively severe / for any person*
> *who lays among them*

ōs byþ ordfruma ælcre sprǣce
wīsdōmes wraþu and wītena frōfur
and eorla gehwām ēadnys and tō hiht

> *god is the origin of all language / wisdom's foundation*
> *and wise man's comfort / and to every*
> *hero blessing and hope*

rād byþ on recyde rinca gehwylcum
sēfte and swīþhwæt ðām ðe sitteþ onufan
mēare mægenheardum ofer mīlpaþas

> *riding is for every man in the hall / easy,*
> *and strenuous for him who sits upon / a powerful*
> *horse along the long paths*

cēn byþ cwicera gehwām cūþ on fȳre
blāc and beorhtlīc; byrneþ oftust
ðǣr hī æþelingas inne restaþ

> *torch is known to each living being by fire*
> *radiant and bright, it usually burns*
> *where nobles rest indoors*

gyfu gumena byþ gleng and herenys
wraþu and wyrþscipe and wræcna gehwām
ār and ætwist ðe byþ ōþra lēas

> *gift is an honour and grace of men / a support*
> *and adornment, and for any exile / mercy*
> *and sustenance when he has no other*

46

wyn ne brūceþ ðe can wēana lȳt
sāres and sorge and him sylfa hæfþ
blǣd and blysse and ēac byrga geniht

> *happiness he cannot enjoy who knows*
> *little woe / pain and sorrow, and has for himself /*
> *wealth and joy, and sufficient protection too*

hægl byþ hwītust corna hwyrft hit of heofenes lyfte
wealcaþ hit windes scūra weorþeþ hit tōwætere syððan

> *hail is whitest of corn, from heaven's height*
> *it whirls, / winds blow it, it*
> *becomes water after*

nȳd byþ nearu on brēostan weorþeþ hī ðēah oft niþa bearnum
tō helpe and tō hǣle gehwǣþre gif hī his hlystaþ ǣror

> *need is hard on the heart, yet for men's sons*
> *it often becomes / a help and healing*
> *if they heed it before*

īs byþ oferceald ungemetum slidor
glisnaþ glæshlūttur gimmum gelīcust
flōr forste geworuht fæger ansȳne

> *ice is too cold and extremely slippery / glass-clear*
> *it glistens most like gems / a floor*
> *made of frost, fair in appearance*

gēr byþ gumena hiht ðon god lǣteþ
hālig heofenes cyning hrūsan syllan
beorhte blēda beornum and ðearfum

> *harvest is men's hope when god allows /*
> *-holy king of heaven – the earth*
> *to give up / fair fruits to warriors and to wretches*

ēoh byþ ūtan unsmēþe trēow
heard hrūsan fæst hyrde fÿres
wyrtrumun underwreþyd wynan on ēþle

> *yew is an unsmooth tree outside / hard,*
> *earthfast, fire's keeper, / underpinned*
> *with roots, a joy in the homeland*

peorð byþ symble plega and hlehter
wlancum ..... ðār wīgan sittaþ
on bēorsele blīþe ætsomne

> *gaming is always play and laughter /*
> *to proud men...where warriors sit / in the beerhall*
> *happily together*

eolhx secg eard hæfþ oftust on fenne
wexeð on wature wundaþ grimme
blōde brēneð beorna gehwylcne
ðe him ǣnigne onfeng gedēð

> *elk-grass most often dwells in a fen, / grows in water,*
> *harshly wounds / marks with blood*
> *any warrior / who tries to take it*

sigel sēmannum symble biþ on hihte
ðonn hī hine feriaþ ofer fisces beþ
oþ hī brimhengest bringeþ tō lande

> *sun to seamen is always a hope / when they travel*
> *over the fish's bath / until the sea-steed*
> *brings them to land*

tīr biþ tācna sum healdeð trÿwa wel
wiþ æþelingas ā biþ on færylde
ofer nihta genipu nǣfre swīceþ

> *Tiw is one of the signs, holds faith well /*
> *with noblemen, on a journey*
> *is always / above night's gloom, never fails*

beorc byþ blēda lēas bereþ efne swā ðēah
tānas būton tūdder biþ on telgum wlitig
hēah on helme hrysted fægere
geloden lēafum lyfte getenge

> *birch is fruitless, yet bears / shoots without seeds,*
> *is pretty in its branches / high in its spread,*
> *fair adorned / laden with leaves,*
> *touching the sky*

eh byþ for eorlum æþelinga wyn
hors hōfum wlanc ðǣr him hæleþas ymb
welege on wicgum wrixlaþ sprǣce
and biþ unstyllum ǣfre frōfur

> *steed is noblemen's joy before heroes, / a hoof-proud horse,*
> *where about it warriors / rich in stallions*
> *exchange words / and is always*
> *a comfort to the restless*

man byþ on myrgþe his māgan lēof
sceal þēah ānra gehwylc ōðrum swīcan
for ðām dryhten wyle dōme sīne
þæt earme flǣsc eorþan betǣcan

> *man is dear to his kinsmen in mirth / yet each one*
> *must fail the others / since by his judgement*
> *the lord wishes / to commit*
> *the poor flesh to earth*

lagu byþ lēodum langsum geþūht
gif hī sculun nēþun on nacan tealtum
and hī sǣȳþa swȳþe brēgaþ
and se brimhengest brīdles ne gȳmeð

> *water is seemingly endless to men / if they must fare*
> *on a tilting ship / and sea-waves*
> *frighten them mightily / and the sea-steed*
> *does not heed the bridle*

Ing wæs ǣrest mid ēast denum
gesewen secgun oþ hē siððan ēst
ofer wǣg gewāt wǣn æfter ran
ðus heardingas ðone hæle nemdun

> *Ing was first among the East Danes / seen*
> *by men until he later eastwards / went*
> *across the waves, the waggon sped behind, /*
> *thus the hard men named the hero*

ēþel byþ oferlēof ǣghwylcum men
gif hē mōt ðǣr rihtes and gerysena on
brūcan on bolde blēadum oftast

> *homeland is very dear to every man /*
> *if there rightfully and with propriety*
> *he may / enjoy wealth in his dwelling generally*

dæg byþ drihtnes sond dēore mannum
mǣre metodes lēoht myrgþ and tōhiht
ēadgum and earmum eallum brīce

> *day is the Lord's sending, dear to men, / god's splendid light,*
> *joy and hope / to the blessed and the wretched, a benefit to all*

āc byþ on eorþan elda bearnum
flǣsces fōdor fereþ gelōme
ofer ganotes bæþ gārsecg fandaþ
hwæþer āc hæbbe æþele trēowe

> *oak is for the sons of men on earth / a feeder*
> *of flesh, often travels / over gannet's bath,*
> *the ocean tests / whether the oak keeps good faith*

æsc biþ oferhēah eldum dȳre
stīþ on staþule stede rihte hylt
ðēah him feohtan on fīras monige

> *ash is very tall, dear to men, / strong in foundation,*
> *holds its place properly / though*
> *many men fight against it*

ȳr byþ æþelinga and eorla gehwæs
wyn and wyrþmynd byþ on wicge fæger
fætlīc on færelde fyrdgeatewa sum

> *yew bow for every noble and warrior is / a joy*
> *and adornment, is fair on a steed / a trusty piece*
> *of wargear on a journey*

 īar byþ ēafixa and ðēah ā brūceþ
fōdres on foldan hafaþ fægerne eard
wætre beworpen ðǣr hē wynnum leofaþ

> *beaver is a riverfish yet it always enjoys / food*
> *on land, has a fine dwelling / surrounded by water*
> *where it lives happily*

 ēar byþ egle eorla gehwylcun
ðonn fæstlīce flǣsc onginneþ
hrāw cōlian hrūsan cēosan
blāc tō gebeddan blēda gedrēosaþ
wynna gewītaþ wēra geswīcaþ

> *grave is frightful to every warrior / when the flesh*
> *begins inexorably -the corpse- to cool,*
> *to embrace the earth, / the dark as its companion*
> *fruits fall away, / joys pass away, promises fail*

2. The Abecedarium Nordmannicum.

This poem (based, like the two which follow, on the edition by Maureen
Halsall) occurs in a ninth century manuscript of *Hrabanus Maurus*; its
purpose is unclear and its diverse origin is betrayed by the fact that the
runes and their names are Scandinavian (probably Danish) while the poem
containing them is written in a peculiar dialect showing characteristics of
Low German, High German and possibly Jutland Danish as well.

ᚠ (feu) forman   *(wealth) first*

ᚾ (ur) after   *(aurochs) after*

ᚦ (thuris) thritten stabu   *(giant) the third stave*

ᚠ (os) is themo oboro   *(god) is over it*

ᚱ (rat) endos uuritan   *write (riding) at the end*

ᚳ (chaon) thanne cliuot   *then (ulcer) separates*

ᚼ (hagal) ᚾ (naut) habet   *(hail) has (need)*

ᛁ (is), ᛆ (ar) endi ᛘ (sol)   *(ice), (season) & (sun)*

ᛏ (tiu), ᛒ (brica) endi ᛩ (man)   *(Tiw), (birch) & (man) amid [them]*
midi

ᚱ (lago) the leohto   *the bright (water)*

ᛣ (yr) al bihabet   *(yew) closes all.*

3. The Norwegian Rune Poem

This poem dates from the late twelfth century; the original manuscript is now lost. Each line begins with a statement about the rune name, followed by a more or less intelligible gnomic statement often with no obvious link in sense to the first half-line.

ᚠ   (fé) vældr frænda róge;   *(wealth) causes kinsmen's strife;*
           føðesk ulfr í skóge   *the wolf feeds*
                                                                      itself in the wood

ᚾ   (úr) er af illu jarne;   *(slag) is from bad iron;*
           opt løypr ræinn á hjarne   *the reindeer often runs*
                                                                   over frozen snow

ᚦ   (þurs) vældr kvenna kvillu;   *(giant) causes women's sickness;*
           kátr værðr fár af illu   *few are glad*
                                                                      at bad luck

ᚨ (óss) er flestra færða fφr
en skalpr er sværða

*(estuary) is the way
of most farings but of swords [it
is] the scabbard*

ᚱ (ræið) kvæða rossom
væsta; Reginn sló sværðet
bæzta

*(riding) they say [is] worst
for horses; Regin forged
the best sword*

ᚠ (kaun) er barna bolvan;
bφl gørver nán fφlvan

*(ulcer) is the bane
of children; death makes
a corpse livid*

ᚼ (hagall) er kaldastr korna;
Kristr skóp hæimenn forna

*(hail) is coldest of corns;
Christ shaped
the original heavens*

ᚾ (nauðr) gerer næppa koste;
nøktan kælr í froste

*(need) makes for little choice;
a naked [man] chills
in the frost*

ᛁ (ís) kφllum brú bræiða;
blindan þarf at læiða

*(ice) we call a broad bridge;
a blind man needs
to be led*

ᛆ (ár) er gumna góðe; get ek
at φrr var Fróðe

*(harvest) is men's bounty;
I hear that Froði
was generous*

ᚦ (sól) er landa ljóme; lúti ek
helgum dóme

*(sun) is the light of lands;
I bow to holy judgement*

ᛐ (Týr) er æinendr ása; opt
værðr smiðr at blása

*(Ty) is the one-handed god;
the smith is often
[busy with] blowing*

ᛒ (bjarkan) er laufgróønstr
lima; Loki bar flærða tíma

*(birch) is the leaf-greenest
of branches; Loki had luck
in deceit*

ᛉ (maðr) er moldar auki;
mikil er greip á hauki

*(man) is earth's increase;
the hawk's grasp
is great*

ᚠ   (lǫgr) er, er fællr ór fjalle   *(water) is that which as a stream*
     foss, en gull ero nosser   *falls from a hillside;*
                                          but trinkets are golden

ᛦ   (ýr) er vetrgrǿnstr víða;   *(yew) is the winter-greenest*
     vant er, er brennr, at svíða   *of woods; burning,*
                                          it is wont to singe

4. The Icelandic Rune Poem

Evidently based on an original in which some at least of the first half-lines were identical with the Norwegian example given above, the later Icelandic poem has been adapted to assist the aspiring *skald* by giving alternative poetic phrases for the runic head-words. The original manuscript also gives Latin glosses (*fé* is glossed *arum* 'gold') and examples of Norse words for 'nobleman, leader' alliterating with the runes' name e.g. *fylkir, vísi, þengill, oddviti, rǿsir*, etc.

(fé) er frænda róg ok flæðar viti
   ok grafseiðs gata

                    (wealth) is kinsmen's strife
                       and sea's flame
                       and serpent's way

(úr) er skýja grátr ok skara
   þverrir ok hirðis hatr

                    (drizzle) is cloud's weeping
                    and harvest's undoing
  and herdsman's [object of] hatred

(þurs) er kvenna kvöl ok kletta
   búi ok varðrúnar verr

                    (giant) is women's sickness
                    and a dweller on cliffs
       and husband of [the giantess]
                            Varðrun

(óss) er aldingautr ok ásgarðs
   jöfurr ok valhallar vísi

                 (god) is the originater of old
                     and Asgard's lord
                 and Valhalla's leader

(reið) er sitjandi sæla ok snúðig
   ferð ok jórs erfiði

               (riding) is a rider's happiness
                    and a swift passage
                 and a horse's hardship

(kaun) er barna böl ok bardaga
för ok holdfúa hús

*(ulcer) is bane of children
and a sore spot
and a place of putrefaction*

(hagall) er kaldakorn ok
krapadrífa ok snáka sótt

*(hail) is cold corn
and driving sleet
and snake's sickness*

(nauð) er þýjar þrá ok þungr
kostr ok vassamlig verk

*(need) is a bondswoman's hardship
and hard circumstances
and laborious work*

(íss) er árbörkr ok unnar þak ok
feigra manna fár

*(ice) is a river's bark
and a wave's thatch
and doomed men's undoing*

(ár) er gumna góði ok gott
sumar ok algróinn akr

*(harvest) is men's bounty
and a good summer
and a ripened field of crops*

(sól) er skýja skjöldr ok
skínandi röðull ok ísa
aldrtregi

*(sun) is the clouds' shield
and a blazing ray
and ice's destroyer*

(Týr) er einhendr áss ok úlfs
leifar ok hofa hilmir

*(Ty) is a one-handed god
and [the] wolf's leavings
and temples' protector*

(bjarkan) er laugat lim ok lítit
tré ok ungsamligr viðr

*(birch) is a leaf-bearing branch and
a slender tree
and a youthful wood*

(maðr) er manns gaman ok
moldar auki ok skipa
skreytir

*(man) is man's delight
and earth's increase
and ships' adorner*

(lögr) er vellanda vatn ok víðr
ketill ok glömmunga grund

*(water) is a welling stream
and a wide gush
and fishes' seabed*

(ýr) er bendr bogi ok brotgjarnt
járn ok fifu fárbauti

*(yew) is a bent bow
and a brittle tool
and arrow's lightning*

three

SEVEN OLD ENGLISH
RUNIC VERSES

1. The Runic Signatures of Cynewulf

The Anglo-Saxon poet Cynewulf is almost unique in the English Christian poetic tradition in that he actually put his name to his verses, although he did this in a most ingenious way. Old English poetry featured alliteration as well as metrical patterning, and this poet manipulated his verse to include the words (which were the rune-names) necessary to spell his name, i.e. *cēn*, *ȳr*, *nȳd*, etc. Lest any reader should miss the point, the words themselves do not appear in the text, but only the runes.

Cynewulf's purpose may have been to ensure that his name would be remembered after his death, so that later generations would pray for his soul. In any event, he succeeded in keeping his name before the public in as much as there has in modern times been much scholarly debate as to whether he could have written any of the other OE poems not bearing his signature: at one time he was credited with many other works, but better critical techniques have shown that those four poems directly attributable to him from the signatures form a cohesive group and have certain common stylistic features. In *The Fates of the Apostles*, Cynewulf playfully challenges the sharp-minded reader to crack the code.

The titles of the poems are the standard modern ones – no OE poems are known to have had contemporary titles – and they appear in two separate manuscripts.

(a) The Fates of the Apostles

Lines 96–106. Vercelli Book, folio 54 recto.

Hēr mæg findan foreþances glēaw
se ðe hine lysteð lēoðgiddunga
hwā þās fitte fēgde ·ᚠ· þǣr on ende standeþ
eorlas þæs on eorðan brūcaþ ne mōton hīe āwā ætsomne
woruldwunigende ·ᚹ· sceal gedrēosan
·ᚢ· on ēðle æfter tōhrēosan
lǣne līces frætewa efne swā ·ᛚ· tōglīdeð.
Þonne ·ᚳ· ond ·ᛦ· cræftes nēotað
nihtes nearowe on him ·ᚾ· līgeð
cyninges þēodōm. Nū ðū cunnan miht
hwā on þām wordum wæs werum oncȳðig

> *Here the man wise in deliberation may find*
> *– he to whom songs are pleasurable –*
> *who made these verses: F(wealth) stands there at the end*
> *– heroes enjoy that on earth, but they cannot always do so together*
> *living in the world. W(pleasure) must fall away,*
> *U(our [things]) in the homeland afterwards fall apart,*
> *the body's passing trappings, just as L(water) flows away.*
> *Then C(torch) and Y(bow) use their skill*
> *in the night's dangers – on them N(need) lies,*
> *the king's service. Now you can tell*
> *who was made known to men in these words*

(b) Elene

Lines 1256 – 71. Vercelli Book, folio 133 recto.

...ā wæs secg oððæt
cnyssed cearwelmum ·ᚳ· drūsende
þēah hē on medohealle māðmas þege
æplede gold. ·ᛦ· gnornode
·ᚾ· gefēra nearusorge drēah
enge rūne þær him ·ᛗ· fore

mīlpaðas mæt mōdig þrægde
wīrum gewlenced. ·ᚦ· is geswīðrad
gomen æfter gēarum gēogoð is gecyrred
ald onmēdla ·ᚻ· wæs gēara
gēogoðhādes glæm. Nū synt gēardagas
æfter fyrstmearce forð gewitene
līfwynne geliden swā ·ᛁ· tōglīdeð
flōdas gefȳsde ·ᚠ· æghwām bið
læne under lyfte landes frætwe
gewītaþ under wolcnum winde gelīcost

> *...Until then man was*
> *buffeted by care-waves, a C(torch) failing,*
> *though in the meadhall he might receive treasures,*
> *apple-red gold. Y(bow) mourned,*
> *N(hardship's) companion, underwent dire sorrow,*
> *the constraining rune, where before him a E(horse)*
> *travelled the long paths – the proud one sped*
> *adorned with filigree. W(pleasure) has fallen away,*
> *– play – after years, youth has gone by,*
> *pride of former times. U(ours) was previously*
> *youth's splendour. Now the old days are*
> *passed away after the due time,*
> *life-joys sailed off just as L(water) flows away*
> *driven by tides. F(chattels) shall be for all men*
> *fleeting beneath heaven; earth's trappings*
> *pass away under clouds, most like the wind*

(c) Christ ii

Lines 793–807. The Exeter Book, folio 19 verso

...Ic þæs brōgan sceal
gesēon synwræce þæs þe ic sōð talge
þær monig bēoð on gemōt læded
fore onsȳne ēces dēman.
Þonne ·ᚻ· cwacað gehȳreð cyning mæðlan
rōdera ryhtend sprecan rēþe word

þām þe him ǣr in worulde wāce hȳrdon
þendan ·ᚻ· ond ·ᛁ· ȳþast meahtan
frōfre findan. Þǣr sceal forht monig
on þām wongstede wērig bīdan
hwæt him æfter dǣdum dēman wille
wrāþra wīta. Biþ se ·ᚻ· scæcen
eorþan frætwa. ·ᚻ· wæs longe
·ᛁ· flōdum bilocen līfwynna dǣl
·ᚠ· on foldan.

> *...Of that terror I must*
> *see sin's punishment, as I tell it true,*
> *where many shall be led to a gathering*
> *before the eternal judge.*
> *Then C(torch) shall shudder, shall hear the king speak*
> *– heaven's ruler – say stern words*
> *to those who previously obeyed him little in the world*
> *while Y(bow) and N(hardship) could most easily*
> *find comfort. Afraid, many must there*
> *in that plain await wearily*
> *what, for their deeds, he will ajudge them*
> *of harsh punishments. The W(pleasure) will be gone*
> *from earth's trappings. U(our[things]) for a long time were*
> *cut off by L(water)-floods, a share of life-pleasures,*
> *F(chattels) in the world*

(d) Juliana

Lines 703 – 9. Exeter Book, folio 76 recto
... Gēomor hweorfeð
·h·ᚻ· ond ·ᛁ· Cyning biþ rēþe
sigora syllend þonne synnum fāh
·ᛗ·ᚠ· ond ·ᚻ· acle bīdað
hwæt æfter dǣdum dēman wille
līfes tō lēane. ·ᛁ·ᚠ· beofað
seomað sorgcearig.

> *...In sadness leave*
> *C(torch) Y(bow) and N(hardship). The king shall be stern*
> *– the giver of victories – when, stained with sins,*
> *E(horse) W(pleasure) and U(our [men]) fearfully await*
> *what he will ajudge them for their deeds,*
> *as reward for life. LF (flood-bound wealth) trembles,*
> *sways with sorrow*

2. Solomon and Saturn

This poem exists in two versions, Corpus Christi College, Cambridge MS 422 (known as MS.A) and MS 41 (known as MS.B). The runes, which start at line 89, are found only in MS.A, in addition to the Roman characters, in *The First Dialogue of Soloman and Saturn*. The whole poem is a kind of verse tour of the more arcane regions of Anglo-Saxon experience – bringing in *Libia* and Greece and the history of India, all with strong biblical or Christian interpretations – set in the form of a challenge dialogue between two competitive wisdom-figures, *Saternus* (classical pagan) and *Saloman* (Judaeo-Christian). Saternus refers to *se gepalmtwigoda Pater Noster* "the palm-twigged Pater Noster" (line 12) and Saloman goes on to set out the virtues of the various characters which spell it, whereby these act as friendly warriors who mete out painful punishment to the 'foe' i.e. Satan..

The poem has little to do with 'mainstream' runelore, but does provide an interesting sidelight on the later uses of runes. Contrary to popular belief, runes had no associations with heathen idolatry in the later English Christian mind, and far more runic texts survive in Christian contexts than in pagan ones: the large carved crosses from Ruthwell and Bewcastle; pillow-stones from monasteries such as Hartlepool; the mixed biblical, Roman and Germanic narratives on the Franks Casket.

Lines 84 – 101

And se ðe wile geornlīce   ðone godes cwide
singan sōðlīce   and hine siemle wile

lufian būtan lēahtrum   hē mæg ðone lāðan gǣst
feohtende fēond   flēonde gebrengan
gif ðū him ǣrest on ūfan   ierne gebrengest
prologa prima   ðām is ᚲ.P. nama.
Hafað gūðmæcga   gierde lange
gyldene gāde   and ā ðone grymman fēond
swīðmōd swēopað   and him on swāðe fylgeð
.ᚠ.A. ofermægene   and him ēac ofslīhð.
.ᛏ.T. hine teswað   and hine on ðā tungan sticað
wræsteð him ðæt woddor   and him ðā wongan brieceð.
.ᛗ.E. hiene yflað   swā hē ā wile
ealra fēonda gehwāne   fæste gestondan.
Ðonne hiene on unðanc .ᚱ.R.   ieorrenga gesēceð
bōcstafa brēgo   bregdeð sōna
fēond be ðām feaxe   lǣteð flint brecan
scines sconcan.....

> And he who eagerly wishes the speech of God
> to sing accurately, and wishes for ever
> to love him without deceit, the loathly spirit
> – the fighting foe – he can bring to flight
> if you first bring from above him
> the 'prologa prima' for which P is the name.
> The warrior has a long rod,
> a golden goad, and ever the grim enemy
> he severely strikes, while on his track follows
> A with great strength, and also strikes him down.
> T hurts him and stabs him in the tongue,
> twists his throat and crushes his cheeks.
> E does him harm, as it always means
> to stand firm against any foe.
> Then against his will R seeks him out angrily,
> champion of letters, it soon grasps
> the fiend by his hair, makes flints break
> the demon's legs ...

Lines 111 – 3

Ðonne .ᚻ.S. cymeð   engla geræswa
wuldores stæf   wrāðne gegrīpeð
fēond be ðām fōtum ...

> *Then **S** comes, the chief of angels,*
> *the staff of glory, wrathfully grabs*
> *the foe by the feet...*

Lines 118 – 36

Swilce hiene .ᛦ.Q. and .ᚾ.V.   cwealme gehnǣgeð
frome folctogan   farað him tōgēgnes
habbað lēoht speru   lange sceaftas
swīðmōde swēopan   swenga ne wyrnað
deorra dynta   him bið ðæt deofol lāð.
Ðonne hine I and .ᚱ.L.   and se yrra . ᚳ.C.
gūðe begyrdað   geap stæf wīgeð
biterne brōgan   bīgað sōna
helle hæftling   ðæt hē on hinder gǣð.
Ðonne hiene .ᚠ.F. and .ᛗ.M.   ūtan ymbðringað
scyldigne scēaðan   habbað scearp speru
atole earhfare   ǣled lǣtað
on ðæs fēondes feax   flāna stregdan
biterne brōgan   banan heardlīce
grimme ongieldað   ðæs hīe oft gilp brecað.
Ðonne hine æt niehstan   nearwe stilleð
.ᚷ.G. se geapa   ðone god sendeð
frēondum on fultum   færeð æfter .ᛗ.D.
fīfmægnum full.....

> *Thus **Q** and **V** make him bow down in death,*
> *the effective folk-leaders travel together,*
> *they have light spears, long shafts*
> *to strike severely – they do not withhold blows*
> *– with harmful strokes; the devil is hateful to them.*
> *Then **I** and **L** and the angry **C***
> *gird themselves for war – the tall letter fights*

> *with bitter fear – soon abases*
> *hell's captive so that he goes behind.*
> *Then F and M throng about him*
> *– the guilty criminal – they have sharp spears,*
> *awesome arrowshot, they let fire*
> *shower its darts in the foe's hair,*
> *a bitter fear; killers sternly*
> *requite in as much as they break their word.*
> *Then at last shall stop him closely*
> *the tall G, which God sends*
> *to the aid of his friends, D travels after,*
> *filled with five powers....*

3. Two Riddles from the Exeter Book

The Exeter Book is a unique collection of OE verse, containing much material of only slight religious interest; our knowledge of the breadth of interest and depth of antiquity of OE verse would be immeasurably poorer had this collection not survived. The Riddles, which are in two sections in the book, are almost our only vernacular record of what was once a popular and important tradition. Several of them have runic aspects, either giving the answer in runes (e.g. *hors*, as mentioned earlier) or using runes to guide and direct the solver. Not all the riddles have a satisfactory solution even today.

(a) Riddle Number 64

Ic sēah ᚱ ond ᛁ ofer wong faran
beran ᛒ ᛗ; bǣm wæs on sīþþe
hæbbendes hyht ᚾ ond ᚠ
swylce þryþa dæl, ᚱ ond ᛗ
gefēah ᚠ ond ᚠ flēah ofer ᛏ
ᚼ ond ᚳ sylfes þæs folces

> *I saw W and I travelling across a plain,*
> *carrying BE; to both on the journey was*
> *H and A the owner's joy*

> *as also a share of strength, Th and E*
> *F and Æ rejoiced, flew across Ea*
> *S and P of that troop itself*

This has been variously interpreted, but there is general agreement that WI stands for *wicg* 'steed' and BE for *beorn* 'warrior', HA for *hafoc* 'hawk', less certainly that ThE stands for *þegn* 'thane, officer' (or *þēow* 'servant'), FÆ for *falca* 'falcon(?)', Ea for *ear* 'sea' (or *eard* 'land'), and SP for *spere* 'spear' (or *spearhafuc* 'sparrowhawk').

Clearly, one could concatenate these runes with possible OE words which might fit the context more-or-less well almost indefinitely. There is no possibility of certainty in the various interpretations advanced so far.

(b) Riddle(s) 75/6

It is not entirely clear from the manuscript layout whether the two sentences given below are intended to be read as two separate riddles or as parts of one, divided by the runes. There are precedents for both practices. I have opted for the latter.

Ic swiftne gesēah on swaþe fēran

· ᛗ ᛉ ᚱ ᚺ·

Ic āne gesēah idese sittan

> *I saw [the] swift [thing] going down the way*
> *D N L H*
> *I saw a lady sitting alone*

Few things better illustrate the subjective nature of OE poetic interpretation than the proposed solutions to this riddle. Apparently, the word recorded in runes has been encrypted by reversing the order of the characters, but HLND is not an OE word in itself so some further work needs to be done. The approach which does least violence to the text is simply to regard the ᚱ as a poorly formed ᚾ and so read the word as *hund* 'dog' – a natural candidate for a fast moving thing on its track, especially if a hunting dog is intended – perhaps the *ides* is waiting for the dog and its master at home? More serious-minded readers have seen the word as *hǣlend* written without the vowels – *hǣlend* is 'saviour', and perhaps there is a reference to some biblical story here. Quite the contrary view is taken by those who read the runes (also supplying the missing vowel) as *hland* 'urine' – something which goes quickly on its way, and also explains the woman sitting alone!

FOUR

ᚦREE RUᚾIC FIᚾÐS FROᚏ BRAᚾÐOᚾ, SUFFOLK

Three objects bearing runes came to light from an excavation at Brandon, Suffolk, and were published in the local history magazine *Gippeswic* along with some extemporaneous but ultimately unhelpful commentary. The following is a re-examination of the texts as published.

I.   The *Tweezer Segment* bears the inscription:

i.e. + ALDRED with the beginning of a further character suggested in the drawing; although the form is indistinct it appears to be no more than the double dot (:) word separator. 'Aldred' is a masculine personal name, here in an Anglian dialectal form not showing the characteristic West Saxon diphthongisation of *a* to *ea* before *l* + another consonant (West Saxon *eald, healh*; Anglian *ald, halh*). The slightly seriffed forms of the runes show the influence of the manuscript tradition and suggest that the item belongs to the mid- to late-Saxon era. The prefixed cross, if not a mere decoration, also puts the inscription into the Christian period. Furthermore, simplification of the vowel in the second syllable suggests a later rather than earlier date: the name is a compound of *ald* 'old' and *rǣd* 'counsel'. It is not clear just when the change (*ǣ* > *e*) took place but it would naturally occur more easily when the vowel does not bear full stress – as in this case, being the second syllable of a compound. Curiously, the name *Aldred* remains in use as a surname to this day.

II. The *Antler* bears a longer text which unfortunately does not mark word divisions and has apparently been worn away at its further end. The runes run

ᚹᚠᚺᛋᛈᛁᚱᛞᚢᛗᛞᛁᛁ ᛁᛁ ᛁᚦᛁ

which may be transcribed thus:

W (?) H S W I L   D   U   M   D (I?)(I?)(?)   (?)   (?)

where (?) marks a character present which is either illegible or unrecognized. There may have been further characters at the end of the text, of which all trace has been lost, although probably no more than about ten since the length of the abraded material is about the same as that of the inscribed section. The penultimate character seems to have consisted of an upright staff and a bow, hence it was probably ᚦ (th) ᚱ (r) or ᚹ (w).

The second rune looks a little like a poorly-formed 'h'-rune ᚺ but is evidently not intended to be identical to the 'genuine' 'h'-rune which follows it. I would suggest that it is an idiosyncratic or inexpertly graven form of the English 'a' rune ᚪ in which the final upstroke which marks out 'a' from 'æ' ᚨ has been extended downwards to meet the lower arm of the rune. This non-standard form may be an early or local variant spelling representing the dialectal development of *æa* or *ea* from *æ*. The standard form (e.g. as on the Thames scramasax) is ᛐ but if the East Anglian dialect produced a diphthong (for example, *æa*) there may have been a local runic spelling convention which represented the sound by means of a modified 'æ' rune ᚨ > ᚪ . It is worth noting that the common Anglo-Saxon runes *æ* ᚨ , *a* ᚪ, *o* ᚩ and *ea* ᛐ are all developed from the Germanic 'a' rune ᚨ.

Accepting this supposition for the moment, two words are immediately discernible: 'wahs', 'wildum'. The first is apparently a runic spelling of what in early West Saxon would appear as *weacs, weax*, the second person singular imperative of the verb *weaxan*, to grow or increase. To interpret '*wildum*' properly we would really need to be able to read the following word clearly, although its form dictates that it must be either a noun or an adjective. If the latter, it is either (i) dative singular masculine; (ii) dative singular neuter; (iii) dative plural masculine, feminine or neuter. If we are dealing with a noun, the possibilities are virtually restricted to the dative plural of a masculine, feminine or neuter noun. Naturally, it could be a substantive, that is to say an adjective used as a noun. The root meaning is evidently 'wild' (adjective) or '(a) wild (thing)' (noun). The use of the dative here suggests instrumentality, since it can hardly be fulfilling its other main syntactic function of denoting the indirect object, as the verb *weaxan* is normally intransitive (it means 'get bigger' rather than 'make bigger').

On a piece of antler, *wild* should refer most readily to the animal from which the object was taken. It is a great pity that the rest of the text is not clear enough to allow a certain reading, although the next word evidently begins with ᛗ 'd', and there is a *prima facia* case for this word having been a form of the word *deor* (beast, animal), presumably the dative singular (West Saxon *deore*). The apparent two 'i' runes after the 'd' rune may then be better interpreted as the uprights of the 'e' rune ᛗ, and the previously mentioned rune consisting of an upright and a bow could equally be ᚱ the 'r' rune. The text would then read:

wahs . wildum. d(eore)
(grow thou, by means of the wild beast!)

Now this bears the hallmark of a charm or incantation focusing the vital energy of the animal into the ritual object, and indeed the whole article may have been intended to be an amulet. From the drawing it is clear that the pointed end has been pierced for suspension from a loop or thong, and it appears to have been incised with triangular motifs at its wider end which may also have had some mystical or religious significance.

III.   The third item is a metal *Pin* with two opposed birds amid interlace decoration on its outer face and a crudely executed runic text on the reverse. The piece dates from the 8th or 9th centuries but the text on the reverse is not the normal ownership formula one would expect from this period. It is obviously the first part of the *fuþorc* although some of the shapes are atypical :

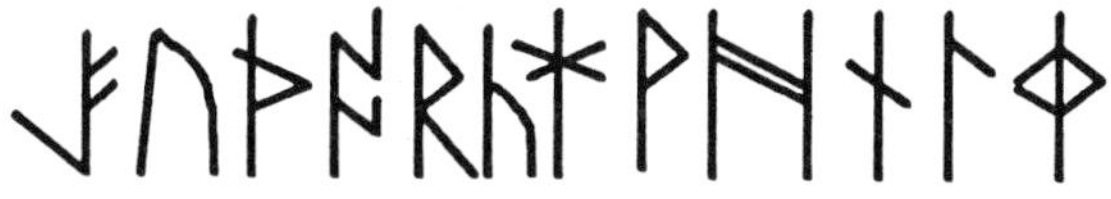

F U Th O R C (G?)W H N (I?) (J?)

1 2 3 4 5 6 7 8 9 10 11 12

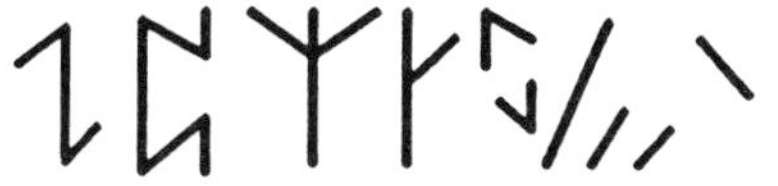

Æ P X (S?) (J?)

13 14 15 16 17

The seventh rune ᛡ would be expected to have the form X which is normal for the 'g' rune. Perhaps the inscriber mistakenly cut an upright stave and was then obliged to correct this as best he could. Alternatively, there may have been a local tradition whereby this shape was normal for the 'g' rune. Certainly in the later manuscript tradition such a form was used for 'j' which in turn may have been used to spell the palatal variant of 'g' occurring before front vowels. An Anglo-Saxon tradition did exist of devising separate runes for this sound (similar to a modern English 'y') which would have been the normal development of the initial sound of the rune name '*giefu*' where the 'g' would have been palatalised – compare the Northumbrian variant ᚸ on the Ruthwell cross.

The eleventh rune should be the 'i' rune but it appears to have an additional arm or cross-stroke which may be no more than an error or chance scratch. Likewise the twelfth rune ᛄ could be affected by the manuscript rune-form which is named 'ger' in Wanley's transcript of the Old English Rune Poem. 'Ger' is evidently 'gēar', again with palatal 'g'. Now in the Germanic rune-row ᛁ 'i' is conventionally followed by ᛃ called ***jera**, meaning 'season' and the ancestor of our word 'year', alluded to by Wanley's 'ger'. There seems to have been a morphological development from ᛃ by the addition of a stave to ᛃ᛫ᛁ and thence to ᛄ here. The addition of a stave to rune-shapes which normally lack this feature has been noted above († from X) for this inscription. The only other known English *fuþorc* inscription – the Thames scramasax – has the form + in this position, which shows no direct development from ⁊ as far as I can determine.

The sixteenth rune Ի ought to have the value 's' although the form here is not the 'standard' one Ⴈ but duplicates that of the Thames scramasax; this shape is also found on the seventh century Chessel Down hilt plate and on the wooden coffin in the tomb of St. Cuthbert. It may be a specifically English form of ⅄ (> Ⱨ > Ի) although the presumptive late date of this pin makes influence from the manuscript letter 'ſ' quite likely also.

The following rune is puzzling since it immediately appears to be a very early (Continental Germanic) form of the rune *jera. One would expect the 't' rune ↑ here and it might be proposed that the staff of the rune has been worn away leaving only the 'head' were it not for the fact that it would be an unbelievable coincidence that a mirror-image of this residual shape should remain from the presumed next rune ᛒ 'b'. It is far more likely that we are here dealing with a late or regional runic tradition in which some confusion of shapes and sequence has occurred. The remainder of the inscription is now illegible.

The pin is pierced on one side, suggesting that it may have been one of a pair or set of three, like those found in the River Witham. I would like very much to know what was written on its sister-pieces – perhaps an ownership formula recording the name of the woman whose dress or headrail it held fast? The surface of the present piece does not appear large enough to accommodate thirty or more runes – in fact there are only twelve in the top line so perhaps twenty-four was the figure to be catered for, the same number as in the Common Germanic rune-row. The curious mixture of apparently early forms (e.g. ꙅ), late forms (e.g. ♢, Ի) and oddities (e.g. †) suggests that here in East Anglia an individual and largely independent runic tradition was developing by the 900s.

As the Brandon pin is one of just two English *fuþorcs* (outside manuscript sources) its importance cannot be overstated, even though it is far from complete. However the divergence between some of its rune-shapes and those found elsewhere only serves to underline the relative lack of interpretable English runic finds we have, and the wealth of local traditions which must once have existed. It is to be hoped that further such finds at new or known sites will enable us to establish a better regional map and typological sequence for our English runic inscriptions.

FOUR

Cbe nORfOLK
'CIW' RUNES
- A RE-INTERPRECATION

(There have been many references in books on runes, Anglo-Saxon religion, and so on, to the TIW runes from the Spong Hill cemetery (above). The *English Heritage Guide to Anglo-Saxon England* published the drawing from which the interpretation was formulated.)

Martin Welch's *English Heritage Guide to Anglo-Saxon England* refers to the pottery found in the excavation of the Spong Hill, Norfolk, cremation cemetery. The funerary urns discovered at that site are interesting in many ways and have been used for typological analysis of Anglo-Saxon pottery. Beyond their importance in the ceramics field, some of the urns bear impressed decoration (illustrated on page 86 of that work) of various types – the quartered circle, the sun-wheel or swastika, the stylized horseshoe and others. The text (page 82) discusses the nature of cremation cemeteries in general terms, as well as the form and function of the urns and their decoration. The author continues: "The more elaborate stamps at Spong Hill include runic inscriptions bearing the name of the warrior god Tiw and portrayals of animals, and it has been argued that these stamp combinations conveyed a message about the person being commemorated." He goes on to suggest that these pot marks are possibly heraldic and are meant to display social information.

Another recent reference to this runic text is in David Wilson's *Anglo-Saxon Paganism*, where the author points out the unique character of the runic stamp which consists of three characters in relief; of the three, the first consists of a T-rune with two pairs of arms, the second a similar form but with only one pair of arms and the third either a bind-rune of I and U or the (separate) y-rune. The interpretation given in this book is of a double rendering of the god's name, whereby the first rune represents the god's initial and the remainder spell the god's name in full i.e. TIU or TY.

What surprised me, turning to the illustration, is that the stamp "bearing the name of the warrior god Tiw" shown in both books actually does not show what one would expect to find as the runic spelling of Tiw's name, i.e. ↑ℙ. The illustration, reproduced above, is taken from the excavation report of the Spong Hill cemetery, and is a good example of a tentative, interim interpretation by an expert in a quite different discipline passing into the 'folklore' of the subject without further investigation (or, seemingly, discussion). The Spong Hill TIW runes are referred to in more than one other book on northern religion and burial practice. I am not sure who suggested that the text in question might read TIW, but it is clear that this interpretation relies largely on the identification of the middle rune with that which customarily stands for the god's name.

Now the text does have as its middle character the spear-shaped rune ↑ which is sometimes used to stand for the whole name *Tiw*, in just the same way as the scribe of the Beowulf manuscript once wrote the 'm' rune (called *monn*, ᛗ) to stand for the word *monn* ('man, person') in the poem. This use of runes as syllabic symbols, which was particularly associated with the riddling poet Cynewulf, was a convenience when the rune symbol could be substituted for the entire word which was its name. The 't' rune ↑ does sometimes appear on English and Continental weapons with presumably devotional intent, the war god's power and protection being invoked through the marking of his name by means of the sign which was itself named after him; the Old English *Rune Poem* clearly refers to Tiw although the manuscript reads *tīr* 'glory'.

But the rune *Tiw* is only one of the three present, and what is more the others are not of regular form. Taking the last ᛜ first, this looks rather

73

like the earliest forms of the *Ȳr* rune whose classic shape is shown as ᛅ ,
but which betrays its origin through earlier shapes: the phonetic value of
this character is a high, front, lip-rounded vowel transcribed as 'y' in
early West Saxon, produced by the influence of the semi-vowel 'i' on a
preceding 'u'. The rune may appear in early texts as ᛁᚢ , transparently a
combination of 'i' ᛁ and 'u' ᚢ. Perhaps, then, the third rune here could
represent 'y'? The dating of the cemetery to the 5–6th centuries makes
this uncertain since the sound change is unlikely to have occurred so early.
Beyond this, it is perhaps stretching the evidence too far to suggest that
the sequence 'ty' could be the same as *Tiw*, though granted in mediaeval
Norse his name can appear with that spelling (the god *Týr*, accusative
form *Tý*).

   And what of the first character? It is not of a recognised early form,
nor does it seem to be a precursor of any later Anglo-Saxon runic shapes I
could discover. If runes 2 and 3 are read as 'ty' the letter before it ought
to be either a vowel or possibly 's', although again this shape does not
closely resemble the 's' rune ᛋ. If instead we must read the
ideogrammatical '*tiw. Yr*' perhaps this first character should be read as a
personal name element, since many Anglo-Saxon names are compounds
of two separate words (e.g. Eadweard < *ead* 'blessed' + *weard*
'guardian'). But no such names consist of three elements; and even if the
first character were merely a determinant or marker signifying "personal
name..." there is the additional objection that no names are known ending
in '-yr', and even the element '*tiw-*' is extremely rare. Regarding the runes
as ideograms or syllabic signs seemed to lead nowhere.

   A further line of enquiry presented itself to me, suggested by the shape
of the first rune ᛏ – it looks a little like a fir tree and reminded me
strongly of the common northern love of cryptography using similar rune-
like symbols (*hahalrunar*). The system is based on the fixed order of the
runes and their respective groupings, known by the Norse name *ættir*.
Traditionally there are three of these groups of eight characters, although
the English extension of the Germanic rune row from twenty four to
twenty-eight signs involved the creation of a fourth group. Any individual
rune can be indicated by showing first its group and second its position
within the group; for example, ᚠ is in the first *ætt* and is the third rune

along so its cipher is ᚠ , or likewise ᛉ is the second *ætt*'s fourth rune, hence ᚨ and so on.

Returning to the Spong Hill inscription, the first sign is clearly of the order 2:2 and the second 1:1. These should indicate the runic characters for 'b' and 'f' respectively. Even allowing for the vowels perhaps not being recorded, this was not a promising start. It might be that the vowels were shown by means of a further cryptic device, namely that of representing them by the following rune in the sequence, a practice known and used in later Anglo-Saxon England. The inscription would then read ᚠ'a/æ' and ᛘ'e' (using the alphabet) or ᛘ'e' and ᚾ'u'(using the *fuþorc*), again improbable as the beginning of an English word even at so early a date. A more fundamental problem was the third character ᚢ, however, which exhibits a rather different shape from the other two; it was clearly meant to be distinct from the sign next to it, but what significance should be attached to the 'branches' reaching down to the base line? This is not a normal feature of the twig-rune system of cryptography, and tended to suggest that another solution to the problem would have to be sought. But what else could these three runes signify? With so little to go on, the problem seemed insoluble.

The answer to the question just posed, when it came to me, had been staring me in the face all along. As often happens, it was necessary to take a step back from the analytical approach I had been following and look again with fresh eyes at the inscription. What I should have seen straight away, before considering the possible phonetic or ideogrammatic content of the text, was its morphology, its shape. What was so striking about the characters before me was that each of them was symmetrical, which few runes are. Could this be chance? Or was there something significant here I had just overlooked? Sure enough, if you bisect each character along its vertical axis (its plane of symmetry) you see a very different text for the stamp now reads ᚨᛚᚢ *'alu'*; moreover, it reads this both forwards and backwards :

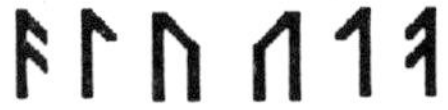

a l u + u l a

What does this mean? Now *'alu'* is not a common Old English word, though it could be an early or dialectal form of the word 'ale' – West Saxon *ealu* or *ealoð*. So was the man in the urn a brewer? A heavy drinker? A licensed victualler? Or could *'Alu'* have been his personal name? In fact as a short formula, *'alu'* is what the Anglo-Saxons called a *galdorword*, a charm or spoken formula. It is presumed to have been in use for some considerable time, since it is found in the elder *fuþark* or Common Germanic rune row (see below). At the early date of the Spong Hill cemetery (C.5–6) it is uncertain whether the first rune would have had its original value 'a' or its Old English value 'æ', but since the word is always spelt with these same three runes it matters little whether we transcribe the earlier *'alu'* or the Poto-Old English *'ælu'*. In fact, the die used to impress the Spong Hill pot must have been of traditional design dating from the earlier runic period – if indeed the stamp itself was not handed down among potters for generations and thus of great antiquity already before it came to England.

According to R. W. V. Elliott, the word *'alu'* (which also occurs on the 3rd century Lindholm amulet and elsewhere) is a 'magic' word of which the meaning is 'protection, taboo'. The similarity of this word to ***aluþ** the reconstructed proto-Norse word for 'ale' caused confusion in later centuries when 'ale-runes' (*ǫlrúnar*) were interpreted as suitable for inscribing on a drinking horn in order to ensure the wholesomeness of the contents. An incident in *Egils Saga Skallagrímssonar* has the hero-runemaster Egil carve ale-runes on his drinking vessel, redden them with his blood and sing a charm over them, whereupon the horn bursts asunder due to the fact that the drink had been laced with poison. Here the nature of the protection afforded by the runes has been re-interpreted and the apotropaic power of the formula *'alu'* has become a much more prosaic litmus test for toxins.

Interestingly, *'alu'* has been encoded most efficiently in an early inscription from Poland (the Korlin gold ring, c.550-600AD) in the form ᚻ . This symbol combines three runic elements: the first ᚠ is 'a' and the second ᚾ is merely 'l' (ᚱ) reversed. But on the *hahalrunar* principle this cipher-shape refers to the first *ætt* ᚱ and second rune ᚠ which is of course 'u' ᚾ; hence 'a+l+u'. So simple and concise a cryptogram must have been a source of great intellectual satisfaction (not to say smugness) to its deviser!

Again, what does *'alu'* mean? According to a survey of the evidence and suggestions carried out by J. B. Conant, it seems to have had a general preserving and protecting function, hence its occurrence on amulets and bracteates. Suggestions as to the history and relations of the word include:

(i)   in the form *aluh* (occurring in one runic text) it could be connected to Gothic *alhs*, Old English *ealh*, Old Saxon/Old High German *alah* all meaning 'temple, sacred place'; we shall return to this notion later, but suffice it for now to say that these terms are all related to the Germanic rune-name ***algiz** 'protection' (ᛉ);

(ii)   an agent noun derived from the reconstructed verb ***alan** 'spring up, arise' with the extended meaning 'growth, prosperity, thriving'; or possibly a form of this verb meaning 'I let thrive, I strengthen, I protect' – this is attractive, especially in connection with (v) below, but seems to lack the essential idea of 'protection' in the phrase;

(iii) under a numericomagical interpretation of the rune-row, ᚠ = 3, ᚱ = 20 and ᚾ = 1, the sum of which is 24 and hence the formula 'alu' stands for all 24 runes; ingenious though this may be, it is far too contrived to command any respect and ignores the fact that 'alu' was evidently a word not a mere cipher;

(iv)   derived from the same ancient (Proto-Indo-European) root as gave rise to the Hittite words *alwanzahh* 'bewitch' and *alwanzatar* 'magic' and the Greek verb *aluein* 'be beside oneself, rage' and perhaps having the meaning 'ecstasy'; this is another idea to which we shall return later;

(v)   simply 'ale', the drink; this is not impossible, since the word often occurs in conjunction with the word ᚱ ᚠ ᚾ ᚲ ᚠ ᛉ ***laukaz** 'leek, onion, garlic' and together the two words may suggest sacred or healing food and drink; yet 'ale' does not fit all the occurrences of 'alu' where something more akin to 'beware!' seems to be involved;

(vi) a trio of rune names **ansuz **laguz **uruz 'god – water – strength' with perhaps mythical associations; this also fails to take account of the fact that 'alu' is a word not a cipher.

Conant himself suggests that *alu = allu* neuter plural of Old Norse *allr* 'all' and means 'all the gods' (which are traditionally neuter in gender in northern mythology). While not without merit, this also seems to fail to capture the apotropaic function of the charm.

As a means of averting bad luck or the effects of evil magic *alu* may have had religious or magical significance. Unfortunately rune magic is so tainted by mediaeval traditions and ideas that it is perhaps unsafe to make any assumptions about what the charm-word *alu* might have meant to the inhabitants of fifth century Norfolk. It is however worth speculating that the word itself is derived from the same Germanic or pre-Germanic (Proto-Indo-European) root as the rune-name *algiz which also appears to mean 'protection'. (If the word were Primitive Old English, '*alu, ælu*' could represent a Germanic noun form *aluz, but this would appear as *aluR in Old Norse, a form which simply does not occur.) Therefore regarding *alu* as a noun of the common type seems quite unprofitable. It is perhaps possible to see it as the first person singular present indicative of a verb, meaning something like 'I protect' or 'I avert (evil)', which form could end in -u. Even in the much later manuscript of *Beowulf* we find such a form as *hafu* for 'I have', retaining the -u ending for the first person singular (line 2523 ...*ic mē on hafu*...). On an amulet this meaning has a particular aptness since it both emphasises the protective power of the object and also renders it 'animate' in the sense that the amulet itself declares its own power.

Alternatively there is a Proto-Indo-European root *alu which relates to sorcery, magic and intoxication, and which lies behind the words 'ale' and 'hallucination' (via Latin from Greek). Another, extended form of this root is *alek with a meaning 'ward off, protect' giving rise to Greek *aleks* (strength), *aleksein* (to protect); and this *alek may also give rise to the Germanic word *algiz (the z-rune's presumed name) with very similar meaning. If the 'alu' charm and the z-rune called *algiz are related, then it may not be overstating the case to suggest that there was some association of ideas in these words. The mere fact that both have a loose connection with protection may mean that their root lies in the PIE root *al- (beyond) – this root gives rise to a great many English words, notably '*al*ter', 'ad*ul*tery', '*ul*timate' etc. from Latin, and the more homely Germanic reflexes '*el*se, *el*sewhere' – with a meaning 'I put (evil) elsewhere, I avert (evil)'. (Against this hypothesis is the fact that the ending -*u* is confined to strong verbs, but the root *al*- cannot belong to this verbal type due to its vowel and root structure.)

Arriving at a substantially similar conclusion by a different route, the noted runologist Professor Elmer H. Antonsen identifies *alu* with Old English *ealoð*, Old Saxon *alo*, etc. all meaning 'beer, ale' and equates 'ale-runes' with 'magic-runes' in that they were perhaps thought to cause delusion and mental excitement, citing parallel Indo-European derivatives such as Greek *alúein* 'be besides one's self', Lithuanian *aliótis* 'rage, act foolishly', and Hittite *alwanzatar* 'magic' (see above).

It is quite likely that the two ideas, 'magic, sorcery' and 'aversion, protection', became merged in the popular mind and a simple verb meaning 'deflect, turn aside, ward off' came to have powerful apotropaic associations which remained into the period of runic development (variously ascribed to the centuries immediately before or after Christ) and gave rise to the concise but evidently time-honoured *galdorword alu*. That this Germanic formula should turn up in fifth century Norfolk should not really surprise us, for the English were then but newly arrived in this island and had not yet learnt to despise their long-standing customs. Whether anyone knew at Spong Hill what the pot-stamp meant is of course another matter, although the presence of runes suggests a rune-master, or at the very least a certain familiarity among those responsible for organising the deceased's affairs with a tradition of runic stamps and dies. By the time the Spong Hill stamp was in use there the meaning might well have been forgotten – especially as the shapes used were not the familiar Anglo-Saxon ones – and its continued use may owe more to family tradition and a feeling of awe attached to some ancient device – a true amulet.

In the aforegoing, I hope I have shown that despite having been accepted by Anglo-Saxonists as a dedication to *Tiw* for more than fifteen years (e.g. L. & J. Laing *Anglo-Saxon England*, 1979, page 87) the Spong Hill inscription must be seen as an encrypted or mystically repeated example of the Common Germanic *alu* formula. How many other disregarded English runic texts await a fresh eye and re-appraisal, I wonder?

Five

The shape of runes to come

Having accompanied me so far through this book, you will probably have formulated an opinion as to what runes are about and you may care to look further into the subject, particularly if you have an interest in the human aspects of history and cannot help feeling a thrill at ancient texts only partly understood. In doing so, you will encounter a problem, in that there are a great many books currently available on the subject of runes, some of which are very good while others are dogmatic and largely at odds with recorded evidence. This confusion stems from the fact that the subject enjoyed something of a vogue during the last and earlier part of this century, and then with the hostility towards everything even remotely German engendered by two World Wars, runes became something of a taboo topic; so much so, that when I took up their study some twenty years ago I could only find two books on the subject, both of which were of very little merit. It is to be regretted that many alleged 'runelore' books published today draw on much the same kind of spurious source material and are no more worthwhile than those early efforts. It can be argued (and often is by those whose interest it serves) that modern attitudes to the runes are equally valid to those of a thousand years ago. And there is some truth in this – we read *Bēowulf*, for example, today and our perception of and attitude to it cannot be identical to that of the poet who sang it or the scribe who first wrote it down; yet we bring a certain set of expectations to the poem and (for many of us) it satisfies them and we consider it as a work of art. Likewise, then, can it not be that we may take up runes and learn from them something of the thought processes of our ancestors, or even of our own? This is an attractive idea but it rather depends on what the author of any given book means by the term 'rune' – and few care to define the term at all. The difference between what I understand as a 'rune' and what is meant by the term in some books is that I restrict its use to any of the characters used in recording the North and North West Germanic languages and their descendants, whereas a more general definition seems to apply elsewhere e.g. 'angular mark used at some time in Europe'. The problem with this is self-evident: if you throw down a handful of sticks at random, the chances are that some of them will fall touching each other, and that many of the arrangements so produced will have been used *somewhere, at some time* as a runic character. It therefore follows that mediaeval masons' marks or guild marks, even the cattle-brands used by American ranchers and the like, which are also often predominantly rectilinear and angular, will often resemble runes. To argue from this for a secret society practising runic magic from Neolithic times into the Middle Ages is misleading and dangerous, and the evidence for it tenuous – though it is not entirely impossible, of course.

The later history of runes – tracing them into modern times – is rather a different subject, touching on Scandinavian and Icelandic folklore traditions and the 'folksy' arts and crafts movements of the last century.

An interesting postscript to mainstream runic studies is in the use of runic – or at least runelike- symbols by the German armed forces during the Second World War. The so-called Odal rune (ᛟ) was the divisional insignia of the 14th Panzer Division, while the 19th used a symbol based on the æ-rune, the so-called *wolfsangel* 'wolf's hook' ⅂, which with variations was also used by Sturmgeschutz Brigade 249, the 2nd SS Panzer Division, Panzergrenadier Division Feldherrenhalle and 4th SS-Polizei Panzergrenadier Division. Naturally, the military elite chose to represent its name (Schutzstaffel) by means of the two initial s-runes: ϟϟ . Closer to home, the party symbol or logo of the Scottish Nationalists is the *ēþel* rune inverted: ⋊⋉ – since *ēþel* is 'homeland' this is presumably no accident!

❁

It seems that runic studies – 'runology' – have now taken two separate paths: one, the academic, inching ahead with painful caution; the other, the popular and 'occult', racing off hither and yon, and often almost entirely lost due to failing to take bearings at regular intervals. And never the twain shall meet, we might think; except that there are a few interested persons whose training and background is firmly academic and who yet are willing to try out other approaches and not dismiss interesting ideas out of hand. It is with them that the future of the subject lies.

ᛉ ᛦ ᛰ

To recapitulate: the runes are a Germanic script of unknown antiquity used for the recording of Scandinavian and North Sea Germanic languages. Much more than this we cannot say with certainty, pending new finds or better analytic methods. It is possible to see symbolic mimesis in some of the rune-shapes, as for example ᛏ as a spear, ᛦ as the outstretched arm warding off harm, or ᚠ as the twin bovine horns, but this approach appears not to be applicable to the shapes as a whole without some very tortuous reasoning. During their almost two thousand-year usage in the north, they have served for all manner of communication purposes – both religious and secular, both magical and mundane – and since the Middle Ages they have been increasingly removed from the ordinary, everyday world and reserved for the magician, the linguistic palaeontologist and the historian. Perhaps one day someone will formulate a 'general principle of runelore' by which all texts may be interpreted; until then, I hope you will agree with me that runes are, above all else, interesting!

APPENDIX 1
Analysis of the Distinctive Features of the Elder Futhark

A **staff** is a basic upright; a **branch** is a single straight line leading upwards off a staff; an **arm** is a single straight line leading downward off a staff; a **crook** is a rightangled turn; a **pocket** is an enclosed area; a **saltire** is an x-shaped cross. (*l* and *r* mean left and right side respectively).

The Common Germanic Rune Row or Elder Futhark

	value	staff	arm	branch	crook	pocket	saltire
ᚠ	f	1	-	2 middle *r*	-	-	-
ᚢ	u	1	-	-	1 top	-	-
ᚦ	þ	1	-	-	-	1 middle *r*	-
ᚨ	a	1	2 top *r*	-	-	-	-
ᚱ	r	1	1 middle *r*	-	-	1 top *r*	-
ᚲ	k	-	-	-	1 middle	-	-
ᚷ	ᴦ	-	-	-	-	-	1
ᚹ	w	1	-	-	-	1 top *r*	-
ᚺ	h, χ	2	1/2 middle	-	-	-	-
ᚾ	n	1	1 middle *r*	1 middle *l*	-	-	-
ᛁ	i	1	-	-	-	-	-
ᛃ	j	-	-	-	1 top *l* 1 bottom *r*	-	-
ᛇ	ǣ	1	1 bottom *l*	1 top *r*	-	-	-
ᛉ	z	1	-	-	1 top *l* 1 top *r*	-	-
ᛈ	p	1	-	-	1 top *r* 1 bottom *r*	-	-
ᛋ	s	-	-	-	1 double (zigzag)	-	-
ᛏ	t	1	1 top *l* 1 top *r*	-	-	-	-
ᛒ	b, ƀ	1	-	-	-	1 top *r* 1 bottom *r*	-
ᛖ	e	2	-	-	1 top	-	-
ᛗ	m	2	-	-	-	-	1 top
ᛚ	l	1	1 top *r*	-	-	-	-
◇	ŋ	-	-	-	-	1	-
ᛞ	d, ð	2	-	-	-	-	1 middle
ᛟ	ō	-	-	-	-	1	1 bottom

84

BIBLIOGRAPHY

The following works were consulted in the preparation of this book, although they reflect only a small portion of the scope of runic studies today.

Toward a New Runic Grammar	Antonsen, Elmer H.	in The Nordic Languages & Modern Linguistics, 1970
The Runes: The Earliest Germanic Writing System	Antonsen, Elmer H.	in The Origins of Writing, 1989
A Concise Grammar of the Older Runic Inscriptions	Antonsen, Elmer H.	Max Niemeyer Verlag, Tubingen, 1975
Interpretation of the Runes on the Gilton Pommel	Bately, J. M.	in Archaeologia, 1967
Anglo-Saxon Manuscripts	Brown, Michelle P.	British Library Board, London, 1991
Old English Grammar	Campbell, A.	Oxford University Press, 1987
Beowulf with the Finnsburg Fragment	Chambers, R. W.	Cambridge University Press, 1948
Runic ALU – A New Conjecture	Conant, Jonathan B.	in Journal of English & Germanic Philology, 1973
The Question of Visigothic Runic Inscriptions Re-examined	Ebbinghaus, E. A.	in General Linguistics, 1990
Runes: An Introduction	Elliott, R. W. V.	Manchester University Press, 1959
Runes, Yews & Magic	Elliott, R. W. V.	in Speculum, 1957
An Early Norse Reader	Garmonsway, G. N.	Cambridge University Press, 1928

Introduction to Old Norse	Gordon, E. V.	Oxford University Press, 1978
Teutonic Magic	Gundarsson, Kveldulf	Llewellyn Publications, St. Paul, Minnesota, 1990
The Old English Rune Poem: a critical edition	Halsall, Maureen	University of Toronto Press, 1981
Altenglisches Etymologisches Worterbuch	Holthausen, F.	Carl Winter Verlag, Heidelberg, 1974
Die Germanischen Sprachen	Hutterer, Claus Jurgen	Drei Lilien Verlag, Wiesbaden, 1975
Anglo-Saxon Runes	Kemble, J. M. (ed. Griffiths, B.)	Anglo-Saxon Books, Pinner, 1991
Anglo-Saxon Pottery	Kennett, David H.	Shire Publications, Aylesbury, 1989
The Exeter Book	Krapp, G.P. and van Kirk Dobbie, E. (eds.)	Columbia University Press, New York, 1936
Anglo-Saxon England	Laing, L. & J.	Routledge & Kegan Paul, London, 1979
Old English – A Historical Linguistic Companion	Lass, R.	Cambridge University Press, 1994
Historical Linguistics: An Introduction	Lehmann, Winfred, P.	Holt, Rinehart & Winston Inc., New York, 1962
Anglo-Saxon Pottery and the Settlement of England	Myres, J. N. L.	Oxford University Press, 1969
The Germanic Languages: Origins & Early Dialectal Interrelations	Nielsen, Hans Frede	University of Alabama Press, 1989
Reading the Past: Runes	Page, R. I.	British Museum Publications, London, 1987

An Introduction to English Runes	Page, R. I.	Methuen & Co. London 1973
The Secret Lore of Runes and other Ancient Alphabets	Pennick, Nigel	Rider Books, London, 1991
Essays in Germanic Religion	Polome, Edgar C.	Journal of Indo-European Studies Monograph, Washington, 1989
Anglo-Saxon Verse Charms, Maxims, & Heroic Legends	Rodrigues, Louis J.	Anglo-Saxon Books, Pinner, 1993
Anglo-Saxon Verse Runes	Rodrigues, Louis J.	Llanerch Press, Llanerch, 1992
Celtic Mysteries: The Ancient Religion	Sharkey, John	Thames & Hudson, London, 1975
Oaks, ships, riddles & the Old English Rune Poem	Sorrell, Paul	in Anglo Saxon England, vol. 19
Handbook of Old-Northern Runic Monuments of Scandinavia & England	Stephens, George	Williams & Norgate, London, 1884 (reprinted by Llanerch Press, 1992)
The Agricola and the Germania	Tacitus (trans. Mattingly, H. revised Handford, S.A.)	Penguin Books, Harmondsworth, 1976
The Etymology of the Germanic Tribal Name ERULI	Taylor, Marvin	in General Linguistics, 1990
And Shall These Mute Stones Speak?	Thomas, Charles	University of Wales Press, Cardiff, 1994
The Anglo-Saxon Minor Poems	van Kirk Dobbie, Elliott (ed.)	Columbia University Press, New York, 1942
Indo-European & Indo-Europeans	Watkins, C.	in American Heritage Dictionary, Houghten Mifflin Co., 1985
Anglo-Saxon England	Welch, M.	Batsford, London, 1992

A Feast of Creatures	Williamson, C.	Scolar Press, London, 1982
Anglo-Saxon Paganism	Wilson, D.	Routledge, London, 1992
The Eastern Front	Zaloga, Steven and Grandsen, James	Arms & Armour Press, London, 1983

Anglo-Saxon Mythology, Migration and Magic

Tony Linsell

The author sets out to cast a spell, and even for your academically hardened reviewer he succeeds. The illustrations are superbly evocative: the text, especially where Runes and Magic are concerned, almost equally so. This is a book to enjoy very much indeed. The Good Book Guide

The author looks at the early North European tribes and their mythology. He traces the migration of some of those tribes to Britain and the creation of the Anglo-Saxon kingdoms that were to merge and become England. During the seventh and succeeding centuries many of the English people where converted to Christianity. Their rich heathen heritage, which extolled loyalty, generosity, vigour and independence, was not totally suppressed by the new religion, despite attempts by the Church to do so. The arrival of Christianity brought many changes but, as elsewhere in Northern Europe, it did not mark a sharp break with the past; instead heathen laws, festivals, magical practices and folk traditions were assimilated into the Christian way of life. Traces of those heathen attitudes, customs and institutions are still with us.

UK £14·95 net   ISBN 0–9516209–6–7   Hardback 21cm x 27cm 144pp

---

Rune Cards

Tony Linsell and Brian Partridge

This package provides all that is needed for anyone to learn how to read runes.

This boxed set of 30 cards contains some of the most beautiful and descriptive black and white line drawings that I have ever seen on this subject.... Pagan News

These are fantastic....Real magic, fabulous and brooding imagery, and an easy doorway to runic realms.... Occult Observer

There is a thick little book which includes clear and concise instructions on how to cast the runes. It is detailed without being overbearing and Mr Linsell obviously knows his stuff.... Clamavi

The illustrations on the cards include prompts that will quickly enable the user to read the runes without referring to the book.

UK £12·95 net   ISBN 0–9516209–7–5   30 cards + booklet

The Hallowing of England
A Guide to the Saints of Old England and their Places of Pilgrimage
Fr. Andrew Philips

In the Old English period we can count over 300 saints, yet today their names and exploits are largely unknown. They are part of a forgotten England which, though it lies deep in the past, is an important part of our national and spiritual history. This guide includes a list of saints, an alphabetical list of places with which they are associated, and a calendar of saint's feast days.

UK £4·95 net   ISBN 1–898281–08–4   96pp

The Service of Prime from the
Old English Benedictine Office
Text and Translation - Prepared by Bill Griffiths

The Old English Benedictine Office was a series of monastic daily services compiled in the late tenth or early eleventh centuries from the material that had largely already been translated from Latin into Old English. From that collection this version of the Old English Service of Prime was prepared for performance at the Anglo-Saxon church of St. Peter-on-the-Wall at Bradwell-on-Sea, Essex on 10th August 1991.

UK £2·50 net   ISBN0–9516209–3–2   40pp

Looking for the Lost Gods of England
Kathleen Herbert

Kathleen Herbert sifts through the royal genealogies, charms, verse and other sources to find clues to the names and attributes of the Gods and Goddesses of the early English. The earliest account of English heathen practices reveals that they worshipped the Earth Mother and called her Nerthus. The tales, beliefs and traditions of that time are still with us and able to stir our minds and imaginations.

UK £4·95 net   ISBN 1–898281–04–1   64pp

Anglo-Saxon Verse Charms, Maxims
and Heroic Legends
Louis J. Rodrigues

The Germanic tribes who settled in Britain during the fifth and early sixth centuries brought with them a store of heroic and folk traditions: folk-tales, legends, rune-lore, magic charms against misfortune and illness, herbal cures, and the homely wisdom of experience enshrined in maxims and gnomic verse. Louis Rodrigues looks at the heroic and folk traditions that were recorded in verse, and which have managed to survive the depredations of time.

UK £7·95 net   ISBN 1–898281–01–7   176pp

Wordcraft
Concise English/Old English Dictionary and Thesaurus
Stephen Pollington

This book provides Old English equivalents to the commoner modern words in both dictionary and thesaurus formats. The Thesaurus presents vocabulary relevant to a wide range of individual topics in alphabetical lists, thus making it easily accessible to those with specific areas of interest. Each thematic listing is encoded for cross-reference from the Dictionary. The two sections will be of invaluable assistance to students of the language, as well as to those with either a general or a specific interest in the Anglo-Saxon period.

UK £9·95 net ISBN 1–898281–02–5 256pp

Spellcraft
Old English Heroic Legends
Kathleen Herbert

The author has taken the skeletons of ancient Germanic legends about great kings, queens and heroes, and put flesh on them. Kathleen Herbert's extensive knowledge of the period is reflected in the wealth of detail she brings to these tales of adventure, passion, bloodshed and magic.

The book is in two parts. First are the stories that originate deep in the past, yet because they have not been hackneyed, they are still strange and enchanting. After that there is a selection of the source material, with information about where it can be found and some discussion about how it can be used.

UK £6·95 net ISBN 0–9516209–9–1 288pp

Monasteriales Indicia
The Anglo-Saxon Monastic Sign Language
Edited with notes and translation by
Debby Banham

The *Monasteriales Indicia* is one of very few texts which let us see how life was really lived in monasteries in the early Middle Ages. Written in Old English and preserved in a manuscript of the mid-eleventh century, it consists of 127 signs used by Anglo-Saxon monks during the times when the Benedictine Rule forbade them to speak. These indicate the foods the monks ate, the clothes they wore, and the books they used in church and chapter, as well as the tools they used in their daily life, and persons they might meet both in the monastery and outside. The text is printed here with a parallel translation.

UK £6·95 net ISBN 0–9516209–4–0 96pp

A Handbook of Anglo-Saxon Food:
Processing and Consumption
Ann Hagen

For the first time information from various sources has been brought together in order to build up a picture of how food was grown, conserved, prepared and eaten during the period from the beginning of the 5th century to the 11th century. Many people will find it fascinating for the views it gives of an important aspect of Anglo-Saxon life and culture. In addition to Anglo-Saxon England the Celtic west of Britain is also covered. Now with an extensive index.

UK £7·95 net   ISBN 0–9516209–8–3   192pp

A Second Handbook of Anglo-Saxon Food & Drink:
Production & Distribution
Ann Hagen

Food production for home consumption was the basis of economic activity throughout the Anglo-Saxon period. This second handbook complements the first and brings together a vast amount of information on livestock, cereal and vegetable crops, fish, honey and fermented drinks. Related subjects such as hospitality, charity and drunkenness are also dealt with. With an extensive index.

UK £14·95 net   ISBN 1–898281–12–2   432pp

Anglo-Saxon Runes
John. M. Kemble

Kemble's essay *On Anglo-Saxon Runes* first appeared in the journal *Archaeologia* for 1840; it draws on the work of Wilhelm Grimm, but breaks new ground for Anglo-Saxon studies in his survey of the Ruthwell Cross and the Cynewulf poems. For this edition, new notes have been supplied, which include translations of Latin and Old English material quoted in the text, to make this key work in the study of runes more accessible to the general reader.

UK £6·95 net   ISBN 0–9516209–1–6   80pp

The Battle of Maldon: Text and Translation
Translated and edited by Bill Griffiths

The Battle of Maldon was fought between the men of Essex and the Vikings in AD 991. The action was captured in an Anglo-Saxon poem whose vividness and heroic spirit has fascinated readers and scholars for generations. *The Battle of Maldon* includes the source text; edited text; parallel literal translation; verse translation; review of 103 books and articles.

UK £4·95 net   ISBN 0–9516209–0–8   96pp

Anglo-Saxon Riddles

Translated by John Porter

This is a book full of ingenious characters who speak their names in riddles. Here you will meet a one-eyed garlic seller, a bookworm, an iceberg, an oyster, the sun and moon and a host of others from the everyday life and imagination of the Anglo-Saxons.

Their sense of the awesome power of creation goes hand in hand with a frank delight in obscenity, a fascination with disguise and with the mysterious processes by which the natural world is turned to human use.

John Porter's sparkling translations retain all the vigour and subtly of the original Old English poems, transporting us back over a thousand years to the roots of our language and literature.

This edition contains all 95 riddles of the Exeter Book.

UK £4·95 net   ISBN 1–898281–13–0   112pp

An Index of Theme and Image to the Homilies of the Anglo-Saxon Church

Robert DiNapoli

For many decades the Old English homilies have been carefully studied for their theological, linguistic and historical content, but they have yet to receive their full measure of attention as literary artefacts (however odd the notion might have seemed to their authors), in part because of the extraordinary labours involved in getting acquainted with them fully. This index is a practical and useful guide to the homilies of Ælfric, Wulfstan, and the Blickling and Vercelli codices, allowing both the researcher and the general reader to range more freely across the mental landscape of these crucial texts than has been possible before.

This is an index and does not contain the texts of the homilies.

UK £9·95 net   ISBN 1–898281–05–X   128pp

An Introduction to Early English Law

Bill Griffiths

Much of Anglo-Saxon life followed a traditional pattern, of custom, and of dependence on kin-groups for land, support and security. The Viking incursions of the ninth century and the reconquest of the north that followed both disturbed this pattern and led to a new emphasis on centralized power and law, with royal and ecclesiastical officials prominent as arbitrators and settlers of disputes.

The diversity and development of early English law is sampled here by selecting several law-codes to be read in translation - that of Æthelbert of Kent, being the first to be issued in England, Alfred the Great's, the most clearly thought-out of all, and short codes from the reigns of Edmund and Æthelred the Unready.

UK £6·95 net   ISBN 1–898281–14–9   96pp

Alfred's Metres of Boethius
Edited by Bill Griffiths

In this new edition of the Old English *Metres of Boethius*, clarity of text, informative notes and a helpful glossary have been a priority, for this is one of the most approachable of Old English verse texts, lucid and delightful; its relative neglect by specialists will mean this text will come as a new experience to many practised students of the language; while its clear, expositional verse style makes it an ideal starting point for all amateurs of the period. The texts are in O. E. with an Introduction and Notes in Modern English.

UK £14·95 net   ISBN 1-898281-03-3   B5   212pp

Beowulf: Text and Translation
Translated by John Porter

The verse in which the story unfolds is, by common consent, the finest writing surviving in Old English, a text that all students of the language and many general readers will want to tackle in the original form. To aid understanding of the Old English, a literal word-by-word translation by John Porter is printed opposite an edited text and provides a practical key to this Anglo-Saxon masterpiece.

UK £7·95 net   ISBN 0-9516209-2-4   192pp

An Introduction to
The Old English Language and its Literature
Stephen Pollington

The purpose of this general introduction to Old English is not to deal with the teaching of Old English but to dispel some misconceptions about the language and to give an outline of its structure and its literature. Some basic knowledge of these is essential to an understanding of the early period of English history and the present form of the language.

UK £2·95 net   ISBN 1-898281-06-8   28pp

We accept payment by cheque, Visa, Eurocard and Mastercard.
For orders totalling less than £5 please add 50 pence for post and packing in the UK.
For a full list of publications and overseas postal charges send a s.a.e. to:

Anglo-Saxon Books
Frithgarth, Thetford Forest Park, Hockwold cum Wilton, Norfolk IP26 4NQ
Tel/Fax: 01842 828430

Most titles are available in North America from:
Paul & Company Publishers Consortium Inc.
c/o PCS Data Processing Inc., 360 West 31 St., New York, NY 10001
Tel: (212) 564-3730 ext. 264

Þa Engliscan Gesiðas

Þa Engliscan Gesiðas (The English Companions) is a historical and cultural society exclusively devoted to Anglo-Saxon history. Its aims are to bridge the gap between scholars and non-experts, and to bring together all those with an interest in the Anglo-Saxon period, its language, culture and traditions, so as to promote a wider interest in, and knowledge of all things Anglo-Saxon. The Fellowship publishes a journal, *Widowinde*, which helps members to keep in touch with current thinking on topics from art and archaeology to heathenism and Early English Christianity. The Fellowship enables like-minded people to keep in contact by publicising conferences, courses and meetings that might be of interest to its members. A correspondence course in Old English is also available.

For further details write to:
The Membership Secretary, Þa Engliscan Gesiðas
BM Box 4336, London, WC1N 3XX England.

Regia Anglorum

Regia Anglorum is a society that was founded to accurately re-create the life of the British people as it was around the time of the Norman Conquest. Our work has a strong educational slant and we consider authenticity to be of prime importance. We prefer, where possible, to work from archaeological materials and are extremely cautious regarding such things as the interpretation of styles depicted in manuscripts. Approximately twenty-five per cent of our membership, of over 500 people, are archaeologists or historians.

The Society has a large working Living History Exhibit, teaching and exhibiting more than twenty crafts in an authentic environment. We own a forty foot wooden ship replica of a type that would have been a common sight in Northern European waters around the turn of the first millennium AD. Battle re-enactment is another aspect of our activities, often involving 200 or more warriors.

For further information contact:
K. J. Siddorn, 9 Durleigh Close, Headley Park,
Bristol BS13 7NQ, England.

West Stow Anglo-Saxon Village

An early Anglo-Saxon Settlement reconstructed on the site where it was excavated consisting of timber and thatch hall, houses and workshop. Open all year 10a.m. – 4.15p.m. (except Yule). Free taped guides. Special provision for school parties. A teachers' resource pack is available. Costumed events are held at weekends, especially Easter Sunday and August Bank Holiday Monday. Craft courses are organised.

Details available from:
The Visitor Centre, West Stow Country Park
Icklingham Road, West Stow
Bury St Edmunds, Suffolk IP28 6HG
Tel: 0284 728718

Short breaks and holidays for Anglo-Saxonists

If you live in the UK and want a short holiday or are a visitor from overseas looking for a place to stay, contact us and ask for details of the accommodation we can provide.

Frithgarth is a 16th century building situated in a beautiful woodland setting on the Norfolk/Suffolk border and is well positioned for those who wish to visit the many East Anglian sites which are of interest to Anglo-Saxonists. (We can provide a visitors' guide.) All those staying with us are welcome to attend the feasts, and other events, we hold from time to time in The Hall at Frithgarth.

Our aim is to help all those who stay with us to get what they want from their visit whether it is to see as many historical sites as possible or to work in the Anglo-Saxon herb garden or to just relax and enjoy the pleasant walks and observe the wild-life of the surrounding forest.

Early English Studies Centre
Frithgarth, Thetford Forest Park,
Hockwold-cum-Wilton
Norfolk IP26 4NQ England
Tel. and Fax 01842 828430